C000000565

GCSE PASSBOOK

COMPUTER STUDIES

Ray Bradley

First published 1988
by Charles Letts & Co Ltd
Diary House, Borough Road, London SE1 1DW

Illustrations: Ian Foulis & Associates

British Library Cataloguing in Publication Data
Bradley, Ray
    Computer studies. – (Key facts. GCSE passbooks).
    1. Electronic digital computers
    I. Title II. Series
    004 QA76.5

ISBN 0 85097 809 2

Printed and bound in Great Britain by
Charles Letts (Scotland) Ltd

Contents

	Page
Preface	4
Introduction and guide to using this book	5
Introduction to GCSE computer studies	6
Hints on how to approach computer studies examinations	8
Sample revision programme	9
1 Getting started	11
2 Input	17
3 Output of data	25
4 Let's keep it	32
5 Flowcharts and all that	37
6 Finding an answer	42
7 Simple programming – the nice way!	46
8 High level languages: climb every mountain!	52
9 Errors: oh no, not wrong again!	56
10 Data processing: large computers do this all day	60
11 Representing data: have a BYTE of this BIT!	66
12 Fields and files	70
13 Low level languages: definitely not English!	76
14 Operating systems: I'm in charge!	81
15 Information retrieval systems	86
16 Systems analysis: is there a better way?	92
17 Computer people: who does what?	98
18 Process control systems and robots	103
19 Applications of computers: look how clever we are!	110
20 More applications of computers: look how clever we are again!	118
21 Applications of computers: we are still being clever!	125
22 Case studies	130
23 Computers and society	135
24 The future: gaze into your crystal ball!	140
Answers to revision questions	144
Final examination advice	156
Index	157

Preface

The introduction of the GCSE means that all students who study the examination called **computer studies** will have covered the same core material. It does not matter where they live in the country, which school they attend, or what examination board they choose.

Computing is a rapidly changing subject and this has been reflected in the change of examination syllabuses in the last few years. We have thankfully gone away from the old mathematical and programming side of computer studies and are now concentrating more on other applications in the real world. Such applications would include word processing, running a spreadsheet or getting information from a database.

Although all the fundamental facts are contained in this book, it is essential that in addition you have experience in the use of computers. This experience usually comes from writing programs and running applications packages as part of your coursework. Indeed, you will have to undertake a project in one of these two areas.

In addition to the computer project you may have to undertake a case study. This is simply a detailed look at some application of computers such as airlines or banks. However, to be able to appreciate these applications fully, you need to go and look at computers operating in business and commerce.

Most secondary schools now have access to several microcomputers at least and also much software to demonstrate applications. You can only gain experience of the sensible use of computers by sitting down and actually using them. This is one of the most important aspects of your GCSE course. Many examination questions can be answered more easily because of the experience that you gain from using computers to solve many different problems.

I wish to acknowledge the assistance given to me in the writing of this book, by Mr David Williams of Farmors' School, Fairford, and his fifth-year computer studies group (1986–7): Mark Betteridge, Martyn Botton, William Bloomer, Caroline Close, Janine Coates, Anne Dix, Elaine Gurney, Sarah Jones, James Mowatt, Robin Saunders, Nicholas Silver, Rebecca Townsend, Jonathan Trickett, Louise Voaden, and Katrina Wilson.

This book provides you with information necessary to understand the core material of GCSE computer studies. The information is given in a clear and concise way and important facts are marked with a special 'K' symbol. Advice is given on how to work out your revision programme.

If you look through the book you will find that the syllabus has been split into 24 chapters. Each chapter is written in four main parts:

1 **Aims** of the chapter,

2 The main text,

3 **Summary**,

4 **Revision questions** (with answers at the back of the book).

From the **aims** you can work out what there is to learn, and from the **summary** you can check that the main points have been covered. When you have finished a chapter the **revision questions** at the end serve as a test to see if you really have understood all the points covered in the chapter.

The material covered in this book represents the **core** of the knowledge that you need for computer studies. In addition to this, especially if you are aiming for a grade higher than C, you will need to know other more specialized topics. It is essential that you find out these from your teacher and include them in your revision programme.

Introduction to GCSE computer studies

There is a set of rules called the **National Criteria** that set out guidelines for all subjects at GCSE level. In addition to these general rules, there are further ones for computer studies. All computer studies syllabuses have been passed because they have been developed with these guidelines in mind.

It has been decided that, for computer studies, you should be able to do all the following:

Section 1. General information processing

You should be able to understand the following terms and ideas:

1 Work out the information requirements of a system in terms of the **output** needed, the **input** data and any **files**.
2 Work out and show in suitable ways, methods of solutions to problems.
3 Describe suitable methods of communicating between people and systems.
4 Explain why **encoding** of data is needed for computer processing.
5 Know what **documentation** is and how to use it.
6 Explain why you need to test solutions.
7 Understand and work out information presented about systems in lots of different ways.

Section 2. Parts of the computer system

You should be able to identify and understand the following **hardware** and **software** for large and small computer systems:

1 Explain what the component parts of computer systems do.
2 Show suitable **input, output** and **storage devices** in particular applications.
3 Explain why we need **interface devices** to enable computers to communicate with other devices, including computers.
4 Describe why we need various **levels** of **programming languages**.
5 Explain the need for **translation programs**.
6 Describe what an **operating system** does and why it is needed.
7 Be able to identify **utility programs** and **applications packages** and say why each are needed.
8 Represent integers, characters and instructions in computer format.

Section 3. Applications of computers

During your course, many of the following applications will be covered:

1 Commercial data processing (e.g. stock control, airline bookings).
2 Technical, mathematical and scientific uses (e.g. civil engineering calculations, date logging, computer-aided design, simulations).

3 Communication and information systems (e.g. teletext, information retrieval, networks and word processing).
4 Process control (e.g. industrial processes, robotics).
5 Educational uses (e.g computer-aided learning).
6 Leisure (e.g. home computers, computer games).
7 Identify the steps involved in the analysis, design, implementation and documentation of a system.
8 Describe different methods of collection, verification and validation of data and the presentation of results and be able to show why the methods for given applications are the best.
9 Describe how data files are organized and used.
10 Explain the need for different modes of computer operation that are suitable for particular types of processing.
11 Identify the tasks of people involved in running the systems.
12 Select and describe some applications to show that you understand all the above.

Section 4. Using computers to solve practical problems

Much of this section may be carried out during the project.

1 Work out the information requirements for the solution of a problem in terms of the output needed, the input data and any necessary files.
2 Encode data and information for processing on a computer.
3 Select suitable methods of communication between people and the system.
4 Work out and test algorithms.
5 Use a computer to make use of the algorithm satisfactorily.
6 Document your work using suitable methods.

Section 5. Effects of using computers

You should be able to argue sensibly about the social and economic effects of the use of computerized systems. Your ideas should show how computers affect individuals, organizations and society.

You should also have a reasonable view of the benefits and drawbacks of using computers.

Hints on how to approach computer studies examinations

Examinations must be prepared for – **weeks ahead**! Remember that you have other subjects that will also need attention. Most successful students make some sort of revision plan that lasts for several weeks. This assumes that you understood the work when it was covered. A sensible revision plan for computer studies is given in the next section.

In computer studies, if you do not get your practical coursework out of the way early, then it is likely to take up some of your valuable revision time. The bulk of your coursework **must** be done well before the deadline for handing in your projects. Make sure that you know this date **months in advance**.

Remember that, although you should work hard on your project, it only accounts for about 25 to 30 per cent of the final marks. This means that 70 per cent or more of the marks are for the final examinations. Do not spend so much time on your project that your revision work for the examinations suffers. (It's no good saying that your project is taking up too much time if you did not start it till very late!).

It is important to set yourself targets: aim to study one chapter of the *Computer Studies Passbook* each day, together with the section of your notes covering the same topic. You will probably find it helpful to have a short break every half hour or so – it is hard to concentrate for long periods of time. It is also a good idea to revise on your own in a quiet place.

You should jot down key words or key ideas as you go along. This will help you to remember things better than if you just read about them. When you get to the end of the chapter, check what you have written down by looking at the summary and then attempt the questions.

You should spend extra time on sections you do not fully understand, even though it might be tempting to miss out the harder topics. Make sure you understand everything in this book – you need to know it.

Computing is not a compulsory subject. You chose to do it. Therefore, hopefully you have some enthusiasm for it. If you have worked hard over the 2 years, done the best you can on your project and worked through a sensible revision programme, then you will go into the examination knowing that you can do your best. Remember, not many people who have put in a lot of effort do really badly.

It is very important to organize your revision so that you can give each subject the amount of time it needs. However, revising for an examination should not mean that everything else stops. You should arrange your work and leisure to fit in together, so that you can have a break from time to time.

This book should help you to organize your revision. It is split up into easily manageable chapters, so it would be easy to learn one chapter each evening. This would take 3 to 4 weeks. Make notes on each chapter as you go along.

When you have gone through the book once, choose the chapters you found most difficult and go through them again. Ask your teacher for help if there is anything you still do not understand.

On the few nights before the examination look through the summaries at the end of each chapter and through your own notes.

Aims of this chapter

After reading this chapter you should be able to:
1 Understand in simple terms what a computer is.
2 Understand the difference between information and data.
3 Explain why data needs to be encoded to be put into a computer.
4 Appreciate what mainframe, mini and microcomputers are.
5 Know the difference between hardware and software.
6 Understand the input, processing, output cycle and the CPU.

What is a computer?

Some people still think of computers as machines that spend most of their time working out long and complex maths problems. In fact, today over 90 per cent of computers spend their time **processing information**.

For example, a customer may need a list of names sorting into alphabetical order. A list of names can be **input** into the computer system, the names will then be automatically processed by the computer and the **output** will be a list of names in alphabetical order. This is typical of a simple processing job that a computer may be set to do. Imagine trying to sort out names into alphabetical order for a telephone directory!

We can therefore see that **a computer is a processor of information**.

There are very few parts of life that can do without information. Examples of information processing include, football scoreboards, newspaper articles, checkouts at the supermarkets, building cars in a factory, flying aeroplanes, getting money from the bank or even playing a game of space invaders. It is therefore not surprising that computers find their way into the above applications and many more.

However, you must not run away with the idea that computers can do everything! **They can't**. At present, computers would **not** be able to judge the winner of a beautiful baby competition, talk about the acting ability of an actor in a play, or control a situation such as a crashing aircraft where many systems could have gone wrong.

Some of you may have noticed the words **at present** in the above paragraph. I have used these words because computers today **are doing** what yesterday would have been thought impossible. The fantastic advances in technology over the past few years have been astounding. Today you will find robots shearing sheep, computers 'understanding' human speech, and computers being used to design other computers.

The difference between information and data

Information and data are important terms to understand. The ideas are very simple. Look at the following numbers and letters:

12BK 9R 3GR 4YL 5BL

Most people would agree that the above numbers and letter are meaningless in themselves. They are simply numbers and letters. Groups of numbers and letters such as those given above are called **data**.

Suppose we are told that the above data represents the number of snooker balls potted in 10 minutes. The code **BK** represents **black** and the code **R** represents **red** etc. We can see that the above data now means that:

12 Black, 9 Red, 3 Green, 4 Yellow and 5 Blue balls were potted.

 When **meaning** is applied to data as in the above example, the **data** becomes **information**.

Encoding information to be entered into the computer

As the computer is a machine, information must be fed into it in a way that the machine can understand. Codes will be represented inside the computer by switching electricity on and off. All information fed into the computer is changed into this 'on' and 'off' form called **binary**. Changing information from one form (such as letters and numbers) into another (such as binary) is called **encoding**.

We can see from the above that **all information must be encoded before it can be entered into the computer system**. The **keyboard** is a simple example of a piece of equipment that does this. Letters, numbers and other special characters are typed in, then electrical signals are sent to the computer. Many other special machines have been developed to encode data and many will be mentioned throughout this book.

Types of computer

There are a vast number of different computers but fortunately they can all be split up into three main types.

1 *Microcomputers*
These computers are the smallest computers and the ones with which most young readers will be familiar. **Microcomputers** are based around an electronic chip called a **microprocessor**. They are found in schools, homes and offices and are used to help out with a variety of tasks from typing letters to doing accounts. The more expensive microcomputers are also found in universities, most businesses and factories. In fact it would be true to say that all types of microcomputers vary from as little as a few pounds to as much as £10 000 for a very sophisticated system. A typical microcomputer system is shown in Fig. 1.

A microcomputer system would probably consist of a keyboard, VDU or monitor (TV-type screen, or keyboard and screen), a disc drive (see later) and a printer. It is usual for only one person to be able to use the machine at any one time.

 2 *Minicomputers*
Minicomputers are much larger and more expensive than

Fig. 1

microcomputers. Such machines are usually found in businesses, banks, departments in large companies and universities. They vary in cost from about £10 000 to over £100 000 for a large minicomputer system. A typical minicomputer is shown in Fig. 2.

It is usual for several people to be able to use the system at any one time because several keyboards and VDUs, called terminals, are often connected to the main part of the computer. A minicomputer will also have equipment such as large discs, tapes and printers connected to it.

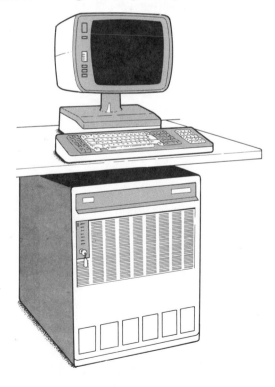

Fig. 2

3 *Mainframe computers*

Mainframes are the largest and most expensive of the computer systems. Even a small mainframe would cost about £100 000 and larger machines often cost several million pounds. The larger mainframe computers are usually found only in the largest of businesses and government departments such as the DVLC in Swansea. However, some of the smaller mainframe computers are to be found in many types of businesses. Mainframe computers also act as the main computer system for universities. The largest and most powerful mainframes are called **supercomputers**. Such computers are often used to forecast the weather. (Not rain again!)

It is often possible for several hundred people to use a single mainframe computer at the same time, and much expensive equipment is connected to the system. It would not be unusual for the computer to be running 6 or 7 large tape machines, 20 large disc drives and 3 or 4 printers at the same time. A typical mainframe computer is shown in Fig. 3.

Unfortunately, as micros get larger and mainframes get smaller, the above arguments get less easy to apply.

Fig. 3

Hardware and software

All the machines that go into making up a computer system such as printers, disc drives, screens and keyboards etc. are called **hardware**. In fact everything that you can touch (e.g. paper, ink, ribbons for the printers etc.) are all examples of hardware.

We have seen at the beginning of this chapter that computers can do a great variety of tasks. This is because they can follow sets of instructions which have been given to them. These sets of instructions are called **programs**. For example, the same computer could be a word processor or play games simply by loading a different program into it.

The general name for all these different types of programs is called **software**.

It is obvious that the computer must remember what it has got to do. This is why it needs a memory as shown in Fig. 4. A **memory** is simply a place where it can store its instructions.

The programs that are being used at the time are stored in the **main store**, but the programs that are not needed (i.e. games that you do not wish to play at the moment) can be stored on **backing store** such as disc or tape until they are needed.

It is most important to realise that **without software computers would not be very useful**. It would be extremely difficult to get them to do even the most simple of tasks. It would be like buying a record player without any records. You have the system that is capable of playing music but no music to play.

Input processing and output

We know that computer systems are very complicated, but all computer systems can be split into just a few main parts. The idea is shown in Fig. 4.

This diagram shows five major parts of the **computer system**. These parts are called **input, processing, output, main store** and **backing store**.

The **data** is fed into the **input**, is **processed** by the **central processing unit** (**CPU**) of the computer and is then **output** on a suitable machine. The **backing store** is necessary if the data is needed by the computer at a later date.

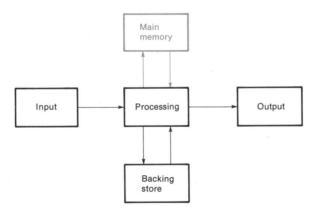

Fig. 4

There is nothing complicated about the above way of thinking. In fact it is quite natural. For example, if you are doing some homework, you can imagine sitting down at your desk as shown in Fig. 5 (overleaf).

The pile of work in the in tray contains the homework questions to be done. These are the input to the system. Your brain then works out what has to be done to answer the questions. This is the processing stage and is similar to that done in the central processing unit inside the computer. Finally, you write down the answers and place the finished work in the out tray. This is the output stage. Backing store might be your reference books. A computer system is, in principle, as simple as this.

16

Fig. 5

The 'magical' processing box
The CPU (Remember what it means?) was mentioned above as the 'box' that carries out the processing. Inside this 'box' there are three main parts. These are the **control unit**, the **arithmetic unit** and the **immediate access store**. Compare this with your brain in the above example. Your brain acts as the control unit, the store and the arithmetic unit. (The last part might not be very good if you don't know your tables!).

The **control unit** of the computer sends out all the signals that control what is going on. The **immediate access store** (or main store) stores all the programs and data that tell the computer what to do. Finally, the **arithmetic unit** is the part that works out and keeps the answers to arithmetic and other types of problems.

Summary

1 A computer is a processor of information.
2 Information is when data has been given meaning.
3 Data must be encoded before it can be entered into a computer.
4 The three types of computers are mainframe, mini and microcomputers.
5 Hardware is the machines: software is programs (sets of instructions).
6 A computer system consists of input, processing and output stages. Main storage (immediate access store) and secondary storage (backing store) will also be needed.

Revision questions

1 Make a list of three things that would be unsuitable for being helped or worked out by computer.

2 Why are computers today able to do much more than the computers of several years ago?

3 Name one device suitable for computer input.

4 Name one device suitable for computer output.

5 What is the difference between **information** and **data**?

6 What does **encoding** mean?

7 Why does information have to be encoded to be entered into a computer?

8 Where would you be likely to find a:

(a) Mainframe computer?   (b) Minicomputer?

(c) Microcomputer?   (d) Supercomputer?

(Lots of possible answers to the above)

9 Name the chip that forms the 'heart' of a microcomputer system.

10 What is the difference between **hardware** and **software**?

11 What is a **program**?

12 Why is backing store needed?

13 What is a **central processing unit**?

14 Name three parts inside the CPU of the computer.

2 Input

Aims of this chapter

After reading through this chapter you should be able to:

1 Understand the problems of data collection.

2 Appreciate the need for different input devices.

3 Understand a variety of input devices.

Data entry systems

You can't put data into a computer unless it can understand it. If the computer can read the data, then we say that it is in **machine readable form**. Examples of data stored in machine readable form would be programs on disc and tape. Often, people have to be able to read the data; which is then in **human readable form**. Sometimes, as in the case of bank cheques (see later in this chapter) the data can be read by both humans and the machine at the same time. The problems of collecting and entering very large amounts of data are enormous. Many machines have been developed so that entering data is quick, accurate and efficient.

Input devices

One basic way of entering data into the computer system is manually by typing it in at the **keyboard** (Fig. 1). However, this is a very slow process in computer terms. Even with a fast typist typing at a couple of hundred words per minute, it is a task that is slow and errors are usually made. Other devices such as the **mouse** (shown in Fig. 1) can replace most of the typing at a keyboard when special instructions have to be given to the computer. This is done by moving the mouse on the desk top so that the pointer on the screen points to a picture called an **icon**. (For example, it might be a filing cabinet.) When you click the button on the mouse, the information you have typed in could be filed on to backing store. This is likely to come into common use. Not only is it quick. but a picture (an icon) is quicker to spot than reading a lot of words.

If a lot of text has to be entered into the computer, you have little choice but to type it in. However, other types of keyboard have been designed such as the **quinkey** shown in Fig. 2, and the special-layout keyboard show in Fig. 3. These special keyboards improve the speeds at which ordinary people can enter data.

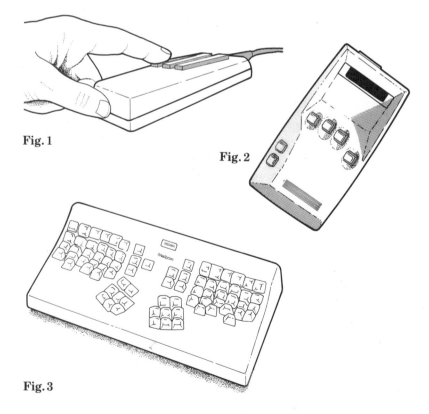

Fig. 1

Fig. 2

Fig. 3

Data capture

Data capture is the name given to the whole process of entering data into the computer system (including collecting it in the first place). One of the problems mentioned above was that of speed. We will now look at some faster methods of entering data into the computer system.

Document readers
It would be very convenient if the data to be entered on a document were already in machine readable form. If this were the case, then typing would not be necessary as the data could be directly read in by a machine called a **document reader**. This is the idea behind some of the following systems. A **document** is simply the name given to the form on which the data is recorded. It can also usually be read by people.

MICR
MICR stands for **magnetic ink character recognition**. It means that characters are written in a special ink that can be magnetized as it is being fed through the MICR reader. Examples of such characters are the strange-shaped writing on the bottom of bank cheques. These are called **E13B** characters and are shown in Fig. 4.

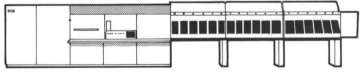

Fig. 4

The MICR characters record such information as bank account number and the branch of the bank etc. A typical MICR reader is shown in Fig. 5. This machine is able to read the MICR characters automatically as the cheque is passed through it. In this way, the MICR reader feeds the data into the main computer system. Without this system, the main banks would not be able to cope with the millions of cheques processed each day.

Fig. 5

Mark sense readers
The MICR characters have the disadvantage that they have to be put on to the cheques by a machine. Often it is convenient to get people to make marks on a form that can be directly entered into the computer system. A typical example of where such forms are used is in examinations. Fig. 6 shows a form which is used to record the answers in a multichoice test.

The examination candidates put a mark (hence the name **mark sense**) in the little boxes. When the form is entered into the reader the marks

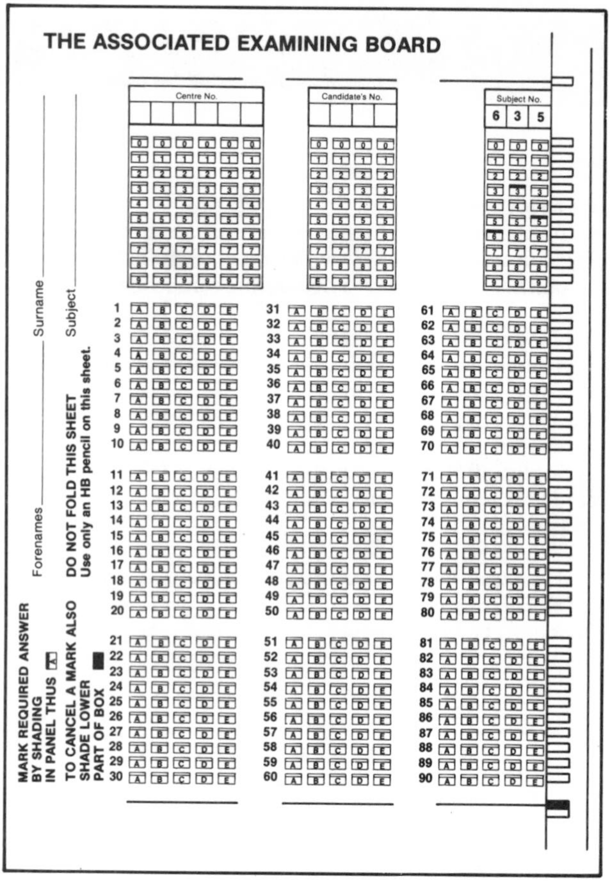

Fig. 6

can be sensed and used to pass information about the candidate and their answers onto the main computer system. It is important that pencil is used or the system may not sense the marks correctly.

OCR Readers

OCR stands for **optical character recognition**. 'Normal' English-like characters can be used. The older OCR readers could only work with very strange-shaped letters, but the latest versions can read a lot of normal typewritten material. They are very useful because a page of typing can be fed into the computer without being typed in at the keyboard.

Turnaround documents

Sometimes, the same form can be used by the computer more than once: For example, an electricity board could make use of a mark sense document where the meter reader pencils in the meter reading.

The form was originally an output from the computer system. That is, information such as customer name and address and account number etc. was put on to the form by the computer.

The customer name and address will need to be in human readable form so that the meter reader can read it, but the customer account number will need to be in machine readable form.

When the form is entered into the computer system again, the computer will automatically know which meter reading belongs to which customer. It can use this information together with the reading to produce the bill.

Documents which are processed by computer and then used to enter data into the computer a second time are called **turnaround documents**. That is they are turned around and entered again.

Bar codes
A typical bar code found on products in the supermarket is shown in Fig. 7. The bar code contains information about the product such as what it is, the size etc. The information can be read by a **bar code reader**. This is a device shaped like a pen that can be scanned across the bars. Also, more sophisticated methods at the supermarket checkout use **laser beams** to scan the bars. Such a device is shown in Fig. 8.

Laser scanners and bar code readers can be used not only to save typing in information at the checkout, but to provide a computer system with detailed information about what is sold. This can be used for stock control purposes.

7808509 765889

Fig. 7

Fig. 8

Fig. 9

Key to store systems

A lot of data still has to be typed into the computer system from a standard keyboard. I have already said that this is very slow. It is not very good if an expensive computer system has to wait while a lot of data is being typed in. (Time is money.) One way to get round this is to make use of machines called **key to disc** and **key to tape** systems. A typical key to disc system is shown in Fig. 9.

This machine enables typists to type data in at the keyboard and the machine (not the main computer) stores the data straight onto disc. This means that all the data typed in can be entered into the computer system much more quickly from the disc at a later stage. That is the computer then reads the information thousands of times faster than someone typing it in.

A key to tape machine is the same idea, except that the data is stored onto tape instead of a disc. The general name for these machines is **key to store** devices. Figure 10 shows the data entry department of a large computer company where many key to store devices are being used.

Fig. 10

Fig. 11

Other data entry methods

Over the years, there have been many specialized data entry methods developed. I will now look at some of them, with typical uses.

Light pen

Fig. 11 shows a picture of a **light pen** being used to pass information on to the computer. A pen-shaped device can be pointed at the screen. Assuming that the correct programs are in the computer, a light-sensitive cell then sends back signals to the computer so that the position of the pen on the screen can be detected.

The way that the light pen is used is similar to the mouse described earlier. A switch on the pen can be clicked so that a point on the screen can be chosen. The light pen can also be used to get the computer to draw a picture on the screen. Typical applications of the light pen are to be found in the section on computer-aided design (see page 122).

Graphics digitizer

A **graphics digitizer** is a machine that can also be used to draw pictures on the screen. However, this time, a more natural process is used because the user draws on a piece of paper with a pencil. The position of the pencil on the paper is sensed by the computer and a copy of the diagram is put on to the screen by the computer. This is a much better and more accurate method than the light pen. It also does not make your arm ache! But it is much more expensive than the light pen. A typical graphics digitizer is shown in Fig. 12.

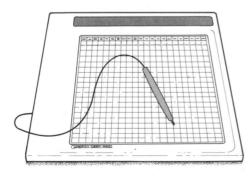

Fig. 12

Touch screen

Touch screen is a method where you can point your finger at part of the screen to get the computer to obey a command. For example a menu may be put up on the screen. You point at part of the menu and a new program might be loaded. This is not the same as the light pen. A special touch-sensitive screen has to be purchased, where invisible beams of light are broken by your finger. A typical system is shown in Fig. 13. A good use would be for young pupils in a primary school. You can imagine the computer asking the child to point to the picture of a cow on the screen. The touch screen could then be used to see if the child gets the right answer.

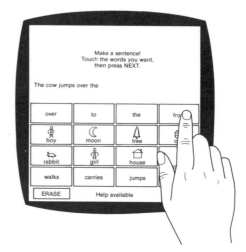

Fig. 13

Speech

Speech is very hard for computers to understand. Many advances have been made, but the big problem is that people all speak differently, even when speaking the same word in the same language. For example can a man from Cornwall understand a man from Yorkshire? Also, the way we use a word can change what we mean. (For example the word 'prime': this would not be the same if we were talking of 'prime beef' or a 'prime number'.)

There are however, systems that can understand a limited amount of human speech.

Summary

1 Data can be in machine or human readable form.
2 Manual data entry (i.e. via the keyboard) is very slow.
3 Many machines have been designed to get data into the computer system quickly and efficiently.

4 MICR, OCR and mark sense readers are used for automatic data entry.
5 Turnaround documents are used to enter data into the computer again.
6 Key to store devices speed up entry of manual data into the system.
7 Bar code readers and laser scanners are used to read bar codes.
8 Special devices such as light pens, touch screens, graphics digitizers and speech are also very useful when necessary.

Revision questions

1 What is meant when data is said to be in **machine readable form**?
2 Name two disadvantages of typing in data.
3 How can a mouse help in entering data?
4 What does **manual data entry** mean?
5 What does **data capture** mean?
6 Explain the term **document reader**.
7 Give one application which uses MICR.
8 Give an application which uses a mark sense reader.
9 Why is OCR useful for entering a page of typewritten text into the computer?
10 Name two devices that can be used to read bar codes.
11 What device is needed to read a multiple choice exam answer sheet?
12 Why might an artist prefer to use a light pen rather than a mouse?

3 Output of data

Aims of this chapter

After reading through this chapter you should be able to:

1 Explain the difference between hard and soft copy.
2 Understand the need for many types of printed output and explain which type of applications are best suited to each output device.
3 Understand why special graphical output is necessary.
4 Understand the need for special output such as COM.

Hard and soft copy

The word **copy** comes from the old printing press days (e.g. newspaper copy etc.). It is now used by the computing industry to mean **a form of computer output**.

K There are many occasions when copy on the screen is not good enough. Such occasions would be the printing of documents and bills, or even to take home a listing of a program you have just written. Any output which is printed out on a printer or plotter etc. is called **hard copy**. Any output which appears on the computer screen is called **soft copy**. Often it is not necessary to generate any hard copy. That is, you may just want to answer a quick enquiry such as the flight time of an aircraft etc.

Printed output

Types of printer
Printers are usually split up by the method used to print the characters. Some printers only print one character at a time. These are called K **character** or **serial printers**. Other, much more expensive printers, print a whole line at a time. These are called **line printers**. Other printers, for example, ones that operate photocopying techniques, can print a whole page at once. These are called **page printers**.

Character printers
Perhaps the most common form of output for microcomputers is the K **dot matrix printer**. A typical printer is shown in Fig. 1.

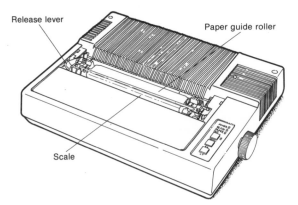

Release lever

Paper guide roller

Scale

Fig. 1

The dot matrix printer gets its name from the fact that the characters are produced from a matrix (group) of tiny pins. The pins are fired by a magnet to hit black ribbon and make a dot on the paper. For example 'M' may be printed in eight or more vertical strips of dots. The more dots, the sharper are the letters. An example of an enlarged character printed by a dot matrix printer is shown in Fig. 2 together with some typical printout.

A typical speed of a dot matrix printer would be about 180 characters per second. Although this sounds fast, it is very slow compared with printers designed to operate with mainframe computers.

The quality of printing from a dot matrix printer is quite good for most purposes, but not good enough to send top quality business letters

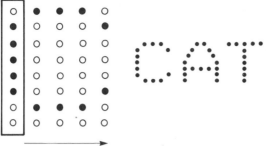

Fig. 2

Direction of print head

that have previously been produced on good electric typewriters. However, the dot matrix can produce a very good quality output called **NLQ** (**near letter quality**), by printing each line of dots a second time after a tiny shift in the paper, and filling in the white spaces between the black dots.

The dot matrix printer is one of the most versatile printers. It can not only alter the style of its characters, but can draw black-and-white reasonable quality pictures. (Called **graphics** in computer jargon.) Again, these pictures would be made up from tiny dots. You can also get seven different colours. Look closely at the newspaper pictures. These are also made up from lots of tiny dots. A dot matrix printer costs only a few hundred pounds. This makes them ideal for microcomputer systems.

Daisy wheel printers
These printers are found mostly in offices connected to word processors (see page 115). They are usually slower in operation than dot matrix printers but give the highest quality print for business letters. A typical **daisy wheel printer** is shown in Fig. 3.

If you look at Fig. 4, you will see why it is called a daisy wheel. The letters are moulded on to the ends of thin plastic strips like the petals on a daisy. These daisy wheels can be quickly changed to alter the style of print. Daisy wheel printers are ideal for use with microcomputers. However, they are slow and cannot do graphics.

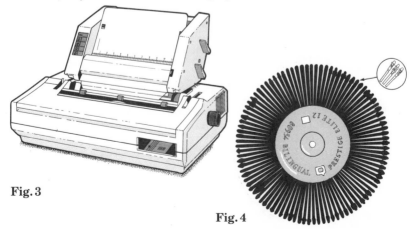

Fig. 3

Fig. 4

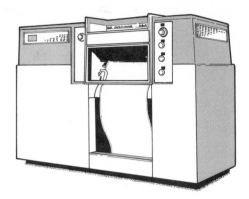

Fig. 5

Line printers

The rate at which mainframe computers can output data is very great indeed. Character printers would be far too slow to cope. For example, if 100 000 rates demands were to be printed, it would take even a dot matrix printer 17 hours to print the bills! (This is going at 180 characters per second and having about 100 or 120 characters for each bill.) A fast **line printer** could do the job in about 30 minutes. A laser page printer (see below) could do the job in about 9 minutes!

If you think the above is fast, the computer could output the same information to a large disc drive in about 5 seconds! A typical line printer is shown in Fig. 5.

Although these printers are expensive, one does not notice the cost too much if you have paid several hundred thousand pounds for the computer which is driving it.

Page printers

Page printers print a whole page at once. A typical **laser page printer** is shown in Fig. 6. The speed with which a fast laser printer can operate is impressive: two million characters per second. Add to this the ability to print photographic quality pictures, and you have a very powerful system indeed. However, they do cost several tens of thousands of pounds each.

Fig. 6

Less expensive (and much slower) laser printers are available to provide excellent quality graphics and text. With the right software, it is possible to produce copy ready for printing.

Graphical output

Although you can get reasonable pictures from a dot matrix printer, or excellent quality pictures on a laser printer, it is not possible to get output suitable for people like engineers, architects or artists etc. Such people often require very high quality, very large graphical output (sometimes up to several metres long by 1 or 2 metres wide!)

Output such as the above can be obtained from what is called a **plotter**. A large **flatbed plotter** is shown in Fig. 7.

A plotter is simply a device that moves a pen across a piece of paper. Most plotters can automatically choose several different coloured pens. Large flat-bed plotters take up much floor space. A variation on the theme is a **drum plotter** shown in Fig. 8. Here the paper revolves on a drum and the pen only moves up and down in one direction as the drum rotates. Smaller A4-size plotters are also available.

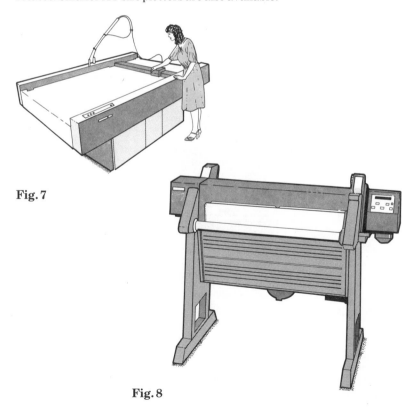

Fig. 7

Fig. 8

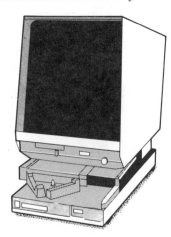

VDU output

The VDU screen (often called a monitor in schools), is a very common form of output. **VDU** stands for **visual display unit**. It is very similar in principle to a TV but the picture quality is much higher. This is necessary so that text can be clearly seen when using 80 columns or more across the screen.

There are also larger special-purpose screens used for high quality graphics output. Such screens are ideal when looking at electronic circuits in detail, or designing new aircraft or cars etc.

Other forms of computer output

COM

COM stands for **computer output on microfilm**. Microfilm is simply photographic film on which very tiny text and pictures can be reproduced. A number of pages of information can be recorded on to what is known as **microfiche**. This is a small piece of film about the size of a postcard that can be placed in a special microfiche reader. Most people are familiar with these machines as they can be found in libraries or the spare parts departments of a motor accessory shop. A typical machine is shown in Fig. 9.

The advantage of such a system is that the information is stored in so little space. Compare this with the room needed to store the same information in normal size in a filing cabinet, and you will be amazed at the difference! The only disadvantage is that you need a special machine to be able to read the information as it is so tiny.

Fig. 9

Speech output

Speech output is very easy indeed to achieve compared with the other problem of speech recognition mentioned in Chapter 3. Many systems are now available that plug into microcomputers to enable the computer to speak. However, at present the vocabulary is quite limited and the

electricity bills etc.). Such processing of information is called **batch processing** as all the information is done in one batch.

Many tapes are often used in very large computer installations. Such tapes are often kept in a special room called a **tape library**. One is shown in Fig. 2.

Fig. 1

Fig. 2

Discs
The main snag in using tape is that you can't go straight to the item that you need. All previous items of data have to be read until you get to the one you want. With disc this is not the case. Data is stored on the **disc** in such a way that you can go directly to the data you require. This method

of accessing data is called **direct access** or **random access**.

On a disc, data can be accessed directly, and discs go round at high speed. So it can be seen that getting data from disc will only take fractions of a second. Compared with this, it can take several minutes using a tape system.

A typical **hard disc** pack has discs made from metal and placed one on top of the other. It contains several disc surfaces (tops and bottoms) on which data can be recorded. Some are shown in Fig. 3.

Fig. 3

Large hard disc machines are really only suitable for large mini and mainframe computers. Here, access to very large amounts of information is required very quickly. (Each disc pack can often store more than 200 million characters of information. Each is available in a few fractions of a second.) An application requiring such speed might be an airline reservation booking system. Disc packs are usually operated in air-conditioned rooms and cost several hundred pounds. The machines in which they are placed are very expensive.

A cheaper alternative to the large hard disc pack is a **Winchester disc**. A typical Winchester is shown in Fig. 4. This system still uses hard discs but they are much smaller. They can only store up to about 30 million characters (30 megabytes or 30 Mb). The rate at which data can be found is also slightly slower. However, these disc drives are considerably cheaper. They cost from only a few hundred to a few thousand pounds. Many are found on the more expensive microcomputer systems.

Floppy discs

This type of disc is totally different from the hard disc described above. **Floppy discs** are made from plastic. They are sprayed with a magnetic coating similar to hard discs and tapes. They derive their name from the fact that they are floppy! They are enclosed in a protective case and come in several sizes. Three different sizes of floppy disc are shown in Fig. 5.

A typical 5¼ inch disc can store up to one million characters of information. A typical floppy-disc drive is shown in Fig. 6. These types of disc form the most popular backing storage for microcomputers. The disc drives can now be purchased for less than £100 and the floppy discs themselves can now be bought for less than £1!

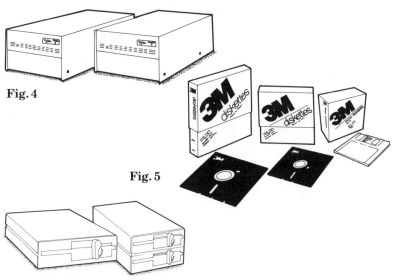

Fig. 4

Fig. 5

Fig. 6

Optical discs
Two of the latest additions to the scene are the optical card and the optical disc. The **optical card** is the size of a credit card and can store one million characters. The **optical disc** is a disc that works using laser light. The storage capacity is a fantastic 2000 million characters of information. Scientists and engineers are having trouble making it possible to record information easily on to disc. Therefore, at present, it is a read only disc. This means that it can only store information put there by the maker of the disc. It is ideal for references like dictionaries and encyclopaedias etc. For example, the BBC Domesday Project uses this method.

Main memory

In addition to backing store it is necessary to have a very fast access store for reasons mentioned at the beginning of this chapter. (Do you remember what they were?) These storage devices are electronic. This means that they have no moving parts inside them. A typical time to get a single item of data from such a store is in the region of a thousandth of a millionth of a second! Although already very quick, speeds are being gradually improved. Main store or immediate access store can be seen in Fig. 7.

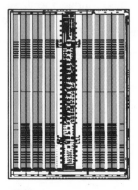

Fig. 7

RAM

The main type of **immediate access store (IAS)** used in computers is called **RAM (random access memory)** for the same reasons that discs are called random access. That is, it is not necessary to have to read through all items of data to get to the one that you require.

The size of RAM inside a computer is one measure of how powerful the system is. (Although it is not the most important.) A typical microcomputer today might have anything between 33 thousand and 5 million storage locations. A typical mainframe will have many millions.

RAM might sound like the best store but it suffers from several disadvantages. Firstly, it is expensive compared with storing the same data on disc or tape. Secondly, the information that is contained in RAM will be lost if the power (electricity) to the system is turned off. This last problem can be overcome by having an emergency battery backup system.

ROM

We often need to store and quickly get information that does not change. For example, when you switch your microcomputer on, it knows how to get characters from the keyboard and display them on the screen. Processes like this are often taken for granted but the computer is following programs that are normally stored in ROM. **ROM** stands for **read only memory**. That is, you can't change what is stored inside it.

EPROM

The data inside a ROM chip can only be put there by the manufacturer of the chip. This is fine if you need thousands of ROMs but impractical if you only want one. A system has been developed to enable small users of computers to program their own chips with a special inexpensive machine. One way of doing this is to make use of a store called **EPROM**. This stands for **erasable programmable read only memory**. Not only

can it be programmed by the user, it can be erased by
using ultraviolet light.

Summary

1 Storage is necessary to store programs and other data.
2 Immediate access store is needed to store quickly needed data.
3 Backing store is needed to store programs and data until required.
4 Discs, RAM and ROM are examples of direct or random access store.
5 Tape is an example of serial or sequential access store.
6 RAM is used for the main or immediate access store.
7 ROM is used to store permanent data.

Revision questions

1 Why do computers need memory (storage)?
2 Why is backing store needed?
3 Why is main store needed?
4 List the disadvantages when using cassette tape as a backing store?
5 Is tape sequential or random access?
6 Why can data be got more quickly from disc than from tape?
7 Why is tape so useful for batch processing?
8 What is meant by direct access?
9 Give a typical situation where the following might be used:
(a) Large hard discs. (b) Winchester disc. (c) Floppy disc.
10 What is the main use for an optical disc at present?
11 What do the letters RAM, ROM and EPROM stand for?
12 Why is RAM not used to store permanent information?
13 What sort of applications programs might be stored in ROM?
14 There is a 2 second power failure. If you are using a computer, would
RAM or ROM be affected?

5 Flowcharts and all that

Aims of this chapter

After reading through this chapter you should be able to:

1 Understand the different program flowchart symbols.
2 Understand a simple flowchart.
3 Solve a simple problem using a flowchart.
4 Know the terms **variable** and **rogue value**.

5 Understand the different systems flowchart symbols.
6 Understand simple systems flowcharts.

Flowchart symbols

K   A **flowchart** uses special symbols so that pictures showing how a problem can be solved are built up. Some flowchart symbols are shown in Fig. 1.

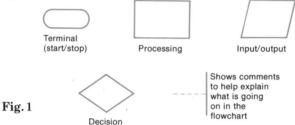

Fig. 1

Simple flowcharts

The easiest way to learn about flowcharts is to use them. A typical flowchart is shown in Fig. 2.

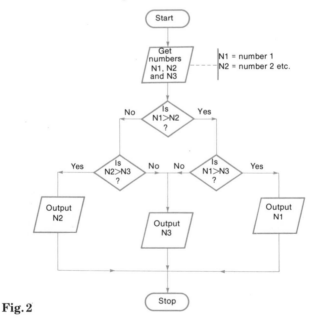

Fig. 2

Start at the top, then work your way through following the arrows on the chart. You **must** do everything that is mentioned in each box **before** moving onto the next. If a question is asked (when a decision box is reached) you must answer the question. Then, depending on the answer you give, leave the box by the **yes** or **no** route.

You should see that the flowchart of Fig. 2 takes any three numbers and finds the biggest. Try 2, 9 and 7. Then try some of your own, including negative numbers.

Variables and rogue values

When going round a loop in a flowchart, a **variable** (strings of letters or numbers that vary) is often represented by a letter or name.

As an example, look at the flowchart in Fig. 3. This shows how to add up the following list of numbers (but not the 999).

2,   4,   9,   1,   5,   3,   999

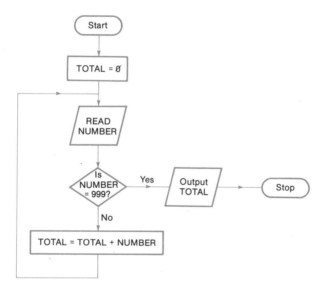

Fig. 3

The variable called 'number' takes on the value of the current number in the list. For example, first time round 2, then 4, then 9 etc. The variable called 'total' increases each time, and represents the total so far. Did you make a total of 24 when you worked through the flowchart?

Notice that at the beginning, when the numbers were being read, we test them to see if 999 has been reached. When it has, we know that we are at the end of the list. 999 does not form part of the numbers to be added. It is known as a **rogue value**.

A flowchart is sometimes used to show how a computer program is worked out. When used in this way, the flowcharts are called **program flowcharts**.

Systems flowchart symbols

Other types of flowchart symbols can help us describe the processing carried out by a computer system in more detail. These symbols are used in **systems flowcharts**. Some systems flowchart symbols are shown in Fig. 4. A typical systems flowchart is shown in Fig. 5.

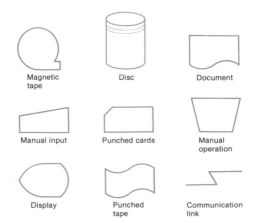

Fig. 4

Magnetic tape   Disc   Document

Manual input   Punched cards   Manual operation

Display   Punched tape   Communication link

The systems flowchart shown in Fig. 5 shows how a computer system could be used to enter data from a keyboard and check for any errors. If the data does contain errors, a report is printed. If the data is satisfactory, then it is stored on disc.

Most of the examples making use of systems flowcharts will need to be done after you have covered work in later chapters.

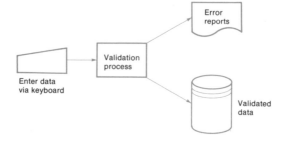

Error reports

Enter data via keyboard

Validation process

Validated data

Fig. 5

Structure diagrams

There are other ways of using pictures to solve problems instead of using flowcharts. A more structured approach preferred by some people is to split up the problem into subproblems. This is a method popular when solving large and complex problems. This is because it enables teams of people to work together on a problem. Each member of the team can tackle a particular subtask. If each subtask proves to be too complicated, then it too may be split up into further subtasks until the problem to be solved is quite easy.

As an example, consider the problem of drawing a pin man shown in Fig. 6. The problem and major subtasks are shown in the structure Fig. 7.

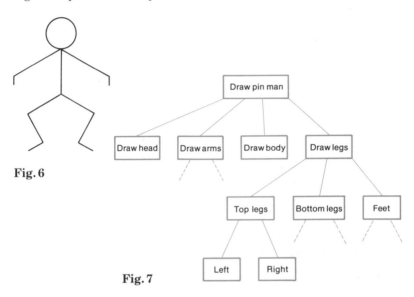

Fig. 6

Fig. 7

Each subtask can then be treated separately as shown in Fig. 7. If a subtask is too complex, then it has been further subdivided into other subtasks. For example to draw the leg, this has been divided into top leg, bottom leg and foot. The structure diagram has no arrows on it like the flowchart had. This is because when each subtask is completed you return to the level above it.

Summary

1 Flowcharts are pictures that show how to solve problems.
2 Flowcharts consist of several basic boxes which make up program flowcharts. Program flowcharts are sometimes used to help write programs.
3 Other boxes are helpful to develop systems flowcharts.
4 Systems flowcharts are useful to describe how a computer system is used to solve a problem.
5 A variable is the name given to strings of letters or numbers that can vary. This is to distinguish them from numbers like pi (3·143) which do not vary. Numbers like pi are called constants.

6 A rogue value is a value to test to see if the end of some data has been reached. Its value must be chosen so that it can't possibly form part of the data.
7 An alternative to the flowchart is the structure diagram.
8 A structure diagram splits up problems into subtasks. If each subtask is still too complex, it is then split up into further simpler subtasks.

Revision questions

1 Draw the flowchart symbols for the following:
(a) Decision. (b) Input/output (c) Terminal (start/stop).
2 What is the difference between a program flowchart and a systems flowchart?
3 Draw the systems flowchart symbols which represent the following:
(a) Disc. (b) Tape. (c) Printout (hard copy).
4 What is meant by a **variable**?
5 Why are rogue values used?
6 Structure diagrams are sometimes preferred to flowcharts, Why is this so?
7 How do structure diagrams help split up large and complex problems into smaller, more manageable ones?

6 Finding an answer

Aims of this chapter

After reading through this chapter you should be able to:

1 Understand why it is necessary to specify a problem precisely.
2 Know why it is important to test solutions to problems thoroughly.
3 Use professionally written packages to solve problems.

Specifying problems precisely (telling them exactly what you want!)

It is important in computing to say exactly what is required when doing a project. If you don't do this, it will often result in the user not getting exactly what is needed. If the problem is not specified exactly, costly alterations may have to be made at a later date. This is a waste of time and money, and will mean that the job is probably not ready on time.

Good communication between all the people concerned is necessary if the end product is to be what the designer intended. This all sounds very grand, let's see what it means.

A good example is in a party game where a chain of people is formed. The first person thinks of a message, whispers it into the ear of the second. The second person then whispers into the ear of the third what they think the first person has said. By the time it gets round the chain back to the first person, it is usually nothing like what it was.

One famous example is:
'Send for reinforcements, we are going to advance'
becomes   'Send for thirty-four pence, we are going to a dance'.

There are many methods to help communicate ideas. Flowcharts and structure diagrams are but two.

Let us consider a simple problem, then look at how effective the solution is. A stock control program is to be written for a retail store. The problem has been split up into several subtasks and you have been asked to do the job of working out the selling price and profits. The following are inputs:

Item	Brief description of each item stocked. We shall use sweets in our example. You decide to call the variable ITEM.
Cost price per unit	The cost per unit to the company in pence.
Quantity per unit	The number of items in a box.
Profit	A fixed profit margin on each item. We shall use a constant of +30 per cent. The cost to the customer is worked out by multiplying by 130/100.
Retail price	The cost to the customer for each item they buy.

Your flowchart for this part of the problem is shown in Fig. 1.

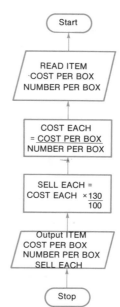

Fig. 1

Testing the solution fully

No problem has been completed until the solution has been fully **tested**. As an example, look again at the flowchart.

To test the solution we need to feed some **dummy data** into the system. The data you feed in should be that to which you already know the answer. That is, we must feed in data that has been worked out properly by hand.

Let us now suppose that the program worked very well for 4 months until a new employee arrived and the following set of data was typed in:

ITEM? .... Mars Bar
COST PER UNIT? 648
QUANTITY PER UNIT? 0

Let's imagine that the clerk did not have the figure handy for the last number and typed in the number '0' for the time being, intending to go back later and put in the correct number. The program crashes, and the computer helpfully announces:

'ERROR NUMBER 18."

Working through the flowchart we get ITEM = "Mars Bar", COST PER BOX = 648, NUMBER PER BOX = 0 and COST EACH = 648/0. It takes an infinite number of zeros to get 648 units! (Try dividing it yourself on a computer if you think it will do it.) After the READ box you would need to add the following, shown in Fig. 2.

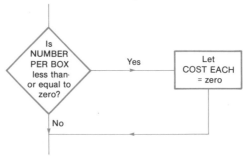

Fig. 2

In real life, systems often go for several years before some unusual combination of data input throws up a problem similar to the above. In practice, more complicated routines could be written to overcome the problem. But you should be able to see why solutions to problems must be fully tested. A lot of work is being done to write programs using mathematical equations so that every possible logic path can be tested, instead of just some of them.

As well as the above problems, if you have written your own program, you will have to sort out all the errors that many be in the program as well!

Using professionally written packages

As can be seen from the above example, writing your own solutions to problems could bring to light many frustrating and time-consuming situations. Many many hours are usually spent ironing out problems in your own software. This could prove to be very expensive.

It is often the case that there is some professionally written software that does exactly what you want. The stock control example above is an application where much professionally written software is available for a variety of computers. Even though this software may cost hundreds or even thousands of pounds, it is often more cost effective than developing your own.

Unfortunately, even if you do buy professionally written software you can't guarantee that it won't go wrong occasionally. However, if it does, you can usually phone up the company who wrote it to get skilled advice and support on what to do.

A **package** may contain a whole set of linked programs, each one using different items from a common data base. So our stock control program might go on to print out a bar chart to show which items are selling well or badly, and then go on to send orders out to suppliers when stocks are low.

Part of your course should involve you in running some professionally written packages. Many of you will choose to do a project on these packages instead of writing programs of your own.

It is often the case that you can do very many worthwhile things using these packages rather than write a few boring and very simple programs which don't get many marks in an assessment.

The range of software packages available is astounding. At any one time there are tens of thousands of packages under development. These packages range from new word processors and other useful things for the office, to specialized packages for companies who design electronic circuits for computers. It is no exaggeration to say that if you have thought of a sensible idea, then someone somewhere has written a package to do it.

Often, you can buy packages that can be tailored exactly to your needs. They might take a little time to set up initially. But once done they can be as good as if you had written the program with your own needs in mind. Also, even if you decide to write your own programs, there are professionally written packages to help you find errors more quickly and easily. There are many **debugging packages** available for languages such as BASIC on many different computers. They are often called **toolkits**.

Summary

1 A problem must be **well explained** if it is to be solved properly.
2 Clear communication between all people concerned is **vital**.
3 The solution to a problem must be fully tested.

4 Using a professionally written package is often easier and cheaper in the long run than writing your own programs.

Revision questions

1 What usually happens if we do not explain carefully how a problem should be solved?
2 Name three typical inputs to a payroll program.
3 What is meant by dummy data?
4 Can we be sure that a complex application written on a computer is completely working?
5 Why is it that sometimes, after years of working correctly, a program can go wrong?
6 A professionally written package, even though it may cost several hundred pounds or more, is often better than writing your own programs. Why is this?
7 What type of professionally written programs can help you to find errors when writing your own BASIC programs?

7 Simple programming –
The nice way!

Aims of this chapter

After reading through this chapter you should be able to:

1 Understand why programs should be written in modules.
2 Understand the following important program ideas:

(a) IF THEN ELSE.
(b) REPEAT UNTIL.
(c) WHILE/ENDWHILE (in some versions called WHILE DO)
3 Know why documentation, a listing of variables, example runs and test data are all important when writing programs.

What a muddle!

Have you ever heard of a spaghetti Western? Well, here is a piece of spaghetti programming:

```
100 READ A$, B
110 IF A$ = "X" THEN 240
120 IF B < 79 THEN 160
130 PRINT A$, "Distinction"
```

```
140 GOTO 230
150 IF B < 59 THEN 190
160 PRINT A$, "Credit"
170 GOTO 230
180 IF B < 39 THEN 220
190 PRINT A$, "Pass"
200 GOTO 230
210 PRINT A$, "Fail"
220 GOTO 230
230 GOTO 100
240 . . . (next part of program) . . .
```

Can you work out what's going on? What is the program supposed to do? This is an example of a program with no structure. There is no easy route through it which everybody can easily understand. It's like a plate of tangled spaghetti.

Look at the program on page 49. It is easy to follow, and has comments to help people understand what is going on. Even if you knew nothing about computers, you would have a good idea of what the program does.

You may not appreciate the need for other people to understand your programs. As long as they work, they must be all right! The first time that you will realize that someone else needs to understand your programs is when you give it to a friend to use and say nothing about how it works, or when a teacher comes to mark them. If they can not easily be followed, then they will be confusing and you will get fewer marks. However, these are not the main reasons.

In industry, very long and complicated programs are written by teams of expert programmers. These projects may take many years to complete. It is likely that people may leave the project before the end. They will need to be replaced by others. At some time, one programmer may have to take over the job of another, right in the middle of writing a program. It is therefore essential that the programs are written in a way that every programmer can easily understand.

It is not possible in the space available to cover many of the actual techniques but we can get an idea of some of the ways it is possible to help other people understand our programs.

Programs written in modules

How would you split up the housework between a number of people? Perhaps it might be as shown in Fig. 1.

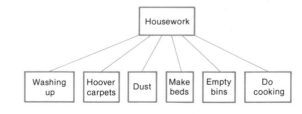

Fig. 1

Having split it up into separate parts called **modules**, it is possible for each person to get on with their own job without getting in each other's way or trying to do each other's job. However, some parts may depend on other people finishing theirs. Doing the cooking is difficult if the washing up has not yet been done!

In a similar way, programs can be split up into modules so that teams of programmers can tackle the job. Each programmer may get a task such as 'write the input routines', or 'write the part that creates the files' etc. When everybody has done their job, it should be fairly easy to join all the modules together so that the whole project works properly. You could not get teams of people to write one long program. They would all be arguing over how each part should be done!

Even when very complex tasks have been split into simpler modules, it is usual to carry on a similar process when actually writing the program. You may already be familiar with **procedures** (or **GOSUBs**; some machines also have named GOSUBs, e.g. GOSUBcheck) when writing programs in some structured versions of BASIC. A **procedure** is simply another piece of program that can be called by name. For example, a procedure may have been written to check that no illegal codes have been used when entering some data. All that might be necessary in your program is to write something like:

```
190
200 PROCEDURE check_illegal_code
210
```

The program is then much easier to understand as the purpose of line 200 is quite clear. The details are taken care of in the procedure (i.e. a separate little module). After the procedure has been carried out, the program will return to line 210 to carry on with the next task.

Making the programs easier to understand

Even when we have broken up a complicated job into lots of simpler modules, we eventually have to write the program. There are good and bad techniques as we have seen from the spaghetti code at the beginning of this section. The use of GOTOs in BASIC is one way of obtaining spaghetti code. To avoid this, several other types of **structures** have been developed. When using these structures properly, good easily understandable code is produced. This is what is known as **structured programming**.

Whole books have written on this subject. The next two or three pages will therefore not be able to turn you into good programmers! However, it does give some examples of better programming techniques.

If then statements

An IF THEN statement is very simple to understand:

IF 'a condition is true', THEN 'do something'.

For example, IF 'it is raining', THEN 'take your umbrella'. Consider writing part of a simple BASIC program which reads in examination marks and prints out whether the result is a fail, pass, credit or distinction using the following table:

Examination mark	Grade
0 to 39	Fail
40 to 59	Pass
60 to 79	Credit
80 to 100	Distinction

In fact, the spaghetti code at the beginning of this chapter does the same job as the following code.

```
100 REM Print out student's name and grade.
110 READ name$, grade
120 IF name$ = "END" THEN 170
130 IF grade < 40 THEN PRINT name$, "Fail"
140 IF grade < 59 THEN PRINT name$, "Pass"
150 IF grade < 79 THEN PRINT name$, "Credit"
160 PRINT name$, "Distinction"
170 . . . (next part of the program) . . .
```

A simple extension of the IF THEN statement is the **IF THEN ELSE** statement. Lines 150 and 160 could have been replaced with:

```
150 IF grade < 79 THEN PRINT name$, "Credit" ELSE PRINT name$, "Distinction"
```

Note also the use of more meaningful variable names. (See later in this section.)

Repeat until loops

This is one of the program techniques that leads to easily understandable programs. An example in a BASIC-type language is now shown:

```
100 REM Number guessing game
110 PRINT "Numbers go from one to ten"
120 REPEAT
130 INPUT "Type in your number", guess
140 Random_number = RND (10)
150 PRINT "I Thought of the number", Random_number
160 UNTIL Random_number = guess
170 PRINT "You thought of the same one as me. Well done"
```

Notice that lines 120 and 160 are shown in bold. This shows the extent of the **REPEAT/UNTIL loop**. All lines between these two limits would be **repeated** over and over again **until** the correct number was guessed. That is the computer would **repeat**edly tell you what number it had thought of and ask you to think of another number **until** you guessed correctly.

Notice that **the repeat until loop will always be carried out at least once**. This is sometimes not convenient if the UNTIL condition is the first to be encountered. This is shown in the following example:

REPEAT
 Tell the dog to sit down
UNTIL the dog is sitting down.

If the dog is already sitting down, then telling him to sit down, even once, is pretty stupid! One way of getting over this problem is to use the WHILE DO structure.

While do structure

Again, this is a simple idea:

WHILE 'I'm in charge' you will DO 'what you're told!'

To get over the problem of the dog already sitting down in the last section we can make use of the **WHILE DO** structure as follows:

WHILE the dog is standing up
 Tell the dog to sit down
ENDWHILE

Make life easy for other people, and yourself!

As you should know from your studies, a **variable** is the name given to some characters in a program that can vary. They are called variables to distinguish them from **constants** which do not vary. Pi (3.143) is a well-known example of a constant.

Programs are easier to understand if you use meaningful variable names. For example, in the spaghetti code at the beginning of this chapter, line 100 READS two variables A$ and B.This does not mean very much in itself. We could look through the program and guess, but can you imagine what would happen if there were 200 different variables? The programer would loose track of what each one did.

To avoid these problems, a list of variables can be given at the beginning of the program. The following might be a typical list using BASIC. Notice that it tells you what each name is used for.

100 REM Variables list
100 REM name$ = student SURNAME from master file.
120 REM grade = Average grade taking all subjects into consideration.
130 REM END = A dummy string to show the END of file has been reached.
140 . . . (etc.) . . . .

Documentation

For many people, the joy of programming lies in getting the thing to work. Most people hate writing down how their program works, or writing instructions that enable other people to use it. When writing professional programs these two requirements are essential. It is also important when writing programs for your projects. A lot of marks will be lost if it is not well explained or the documentation is poor.

Documentation is simply the written material that goes with a system to make it more easily understandable. It is usually split up into different types according to its purpose. For example, **user documentation** would be written to enable people who have to use the system or program to be able to use it very easily. It is generally nontechnical and goes into no detail about how the programs were written etc. **Technical documentation**, however, contains all the necessary detail to enable someone else to modify the program or system at a later date.

Summary

1 Programs **must** be written so that other people can understand them. Other people may have to modify them at a later date.
2 Splitting up programs into modules makes them more easily understandable and enables teams of people to work on separate parts.
3 Making use of REPEAT UNTIL, WHILE, ENDWHILE, IF THEN statements and procedures makes code more easily understood. Don't use GOTOs; it leads to spaghetti programs.
4 Have a list of variables at the beginning of your programs.
5 Use meaningful variable names.
6 Paying attention to all things like those mentioned in **1, 2, 3, 4** and **5** above is called structured programming.
7 Good documentation is essential if people are to understand how to use and possibly modify programs at a later date.

Revision questions

1 Why bother to write programs in easily understandable ways if they work perfectly well?
2 In BASIC, what statement is to be avoided if possible?
3 We often split programs up into modules. What is a **module**?
4 List two advantages of writing programs in modules.
5 What is **structured programming**?
6 What is **documentation**?
7 Why is documentation necessary?
8 Give examples of two different types of documentation.

8 High level languages: climb every mountain!

Aims of this chapter

After reading through this chapter you should be able to:

1 Understand what is meant by a high level language.
2 Understand why high level languages are necessary.
3 Know why there are many different high level languages.
4 Understand the terms compiler and interpreter.

What is a high level language?

You should remember from Chapter 2 that without software (the programs) computers would be very hard to use. There are many different types of software. In this chapter we are going to concentrate on programs that are written in what is called a high level language. Chapter 13 will concentrate on low level languages.

A **high level language** is one that has been designed to make writing programs easier for the noncomputer specialist. They are a little like English, and so are easy to understand. An example of a high level language with which most home micro owners are familiar is **BASIC**. This stands for: **Beginners All-purpose Symbolic Instruction Code**. This was one of the first to be written to help students learn to program in a simple way, making use of English-like statements such as: PRINT, IF, THEN, FOR, NEXT etc.

BASIC is a general purpose language. That is, it has not been designed to do any special tasks such as guide missiles, control robots or quickly search a large store of data.

Why do we need different high level languages

If you have written all of your programs in BASIC, then you may not see why other languages are needed. You must realize that in business and industry there are lots of special things with which BASIC could not cope very efficiently. BASIC would be **too slow** for controlling a missile. BASIC would not have the complex **file handling** necessary to deal with large amounts of data on a mainframe computer. BASIC would be **too complicated** for very young children to learn how to program the computer in a simple way. These are just a few reasons why you need different high level languages.

A very quick tour of some high level languages

We will now look at some common examples of different high level languages and their uses:

COBOL

COBOL stands for: **Common Business-Oriented Language**. It is a language that is used for dealing with large files of information in businesses. Typical examples would be payroll processing or producing electricity and gas bills etc. Most of the programming throughout the business world is done using COBOL. So it is one of the most used commercial languages.

FORTRAN
FORTRAN stands for **FORmula TRANslation**. This is a scientific language that has some special mathematical features that make it useful for engineers and scientists. Although quite old (it was developed in 1956), many versions have been developed, and the latest one is expected in 1988.

Pascal
Pascal is a general-purpose language named after the famous mathematician Blaise Pascal. It has been designed for the teaching of programming in a structured way. (See page 48 for structured programming.) BASIC is often criticized because many versions of it lack any clear shape, but finish up like a plate of spaghetti.

LOGO
LOGO is a simple programming language which can be used by young children to read and write simple computer programs. But it is also useful for processing lists. The best known use is to control a turtle which can draw pictures. Fig. 1 shows a typical LOGO program; and Fig. 2 shows the output that is produced. Notice how no line numbers are used, and how very easy it is to understand, even if you have not learnt any LOGO. However, LOGO also has many other features which make it a powerful programming language in its own right.

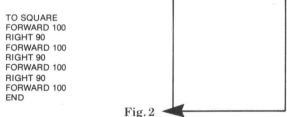

```
TO SQUARE
FORWARD 100
RIGHT 90
FORWARD 100
RIGHT 90
FORWARD 100
RIGHT 90
FORWARD 100
END
```

Fig. 1   **Fig. 2**

We can see that high level languages have been designed for special purposes. It is not possible so far to get one language to do everything that you need. For one thing it would be very complicated for people to develop, and it would need a very large amount of computer memory, a large part of which would not be needed for most of the time. It is more efficient to get a special-purpose language to do most of the things that you want to do for most of the time. But as computers get faster and large memories get cheaper we may end up with a general-purpose language, as the speed will disguise its inefficiency.

What are interpreters and compilers?

We already know that computers work in binary. We also know that high level languages are made up of English-like statements. It must therefore be obvious that something must convert these English-like high level language statements into a code that the machine can understand. This is the job of a complicated set of programs called **interpreters** and **compilers**. First let us look at an interpreter.

Interpreter

The job of an **interpreter** is exactly the same as a language interpreter. For example, if you can't speak French, then you may get an interpreter to interpret what you are saying into French, so that a French person could understand. In the same way, an interpreter on a computer changes each statement in a high level language into a code that the machine can understand.

We will consider the language BASIC as an example. A BASIC interpreter will convert the program you have written **one line at a time** as it is being run on the computer (i.e. as the instructions that you have given the computer are being carried out). While this interpretation is taking place, it will have to check to see if you have made any mistakes. One example of a mistake could be a syntax error. (I expect that you have all come across these when you break one of the rules of the language!) Another example might be making sure that you have beginnings and ends to each loop in your program. All this checking takes a long time. This is one of the reasons why many versions of BASIC are slow.

Compiler

A method to get your BASIC program to run faster is to convert it into code that the machine can understand **all at once**. This happens **before** any of the statements are carried out. This is called the **compilation stage**. Many errors (such as syntax errors) can be checked during this stage.

After the program has been **compiled**, it is then run in the machine code that the computer can understand. It is now ready to be run on the computer. As less checking is now going on, the program will run much faster than the interpreted version.

If compiled programs run much faster than interpreted programs, you may wonder why compilers are not used all the time. In fact interpreters make it much easier for the computer user to change any mistakes that may have been made. You can usually change a line of your BASIC program by retyping it, or using the simple line editor on your computer. If you have a compiler, then, even if only a single mistake has been found, the whole program will have to be recompiled before it can be run again. This is a much more complex process, and if done takes a lot of time.

Most high level languages used professionally such as FORTRAN, COBOL, and Pascal etc. are compiled. Some versions of BASIC are also compiled.

Summary

1 High level languages allow you to write programs in simple English-like ways that make programming the computer fairly easy.

2 Different high level languages are needed to do many different tasks more efficiently (e.g. the needs of accountants and engineers would be very different).

3 Some different high level languages are:

COBOL ....used in business;
FORTRAN..........used in engineering and science;
Pascal...................developed for structured programming teaching;
LOGO ....used to teach young children how to program;
BASIC..................a general-purpose, easy to learn language for students.

4 High level languages need to be converted into a form that the computer can understand. Compilers and interpreters do this.

5 An interpreter converts one line of a high level language at a time, and so is very slow. However, it is easy to use.

6 A compiler converts all of the program into code once and for all before the program is run. It is much faster than an interpreter but is more complicated to use.

Revision questions

1 What is meant by a high level language?

2 Why is BASIC not the only high level language?

3 Give one advantage of using a high level language.

4 Why is BASIC very slow compared with some other high level languages?

5 BASIC is often interpreted. What does this mean?

6 Why is a compiled BASIC program faster than an interpreted BASIC program?

7 Why are compilers and interpreters needed?

8 Name two high level languages other than BASIC. What is the main use of the two languages you have used?

9 Name a high level language that is especially useful for teaching very young children how to program a computer?

10 A large computer runs a payroll program the day before payday. Which language is it likely to be written in? If a bug is found later, how will the program writers produce a new version?

9 Errors: oh no, not wrong again!

Aims of this chapter

After reading through this chapter you should be able to:

1 Understand what is meant by an error.
2 Know that there are different types of errors.
3 Understand some of the methods used for reducing errors.
4 Understand the terms verification and validation.

What are errors?

I expect that you have all read stories in the press when an old person living by themselves receives an electricity bill for £1 000 000. Many people laugh and say what stupid machines computers are. In fact, it is not usually the **computer** that has gone wrong, but an error in the way that the computer system has been **operated**.

In this chapter, we will take a brief look at how some errors might occur, and some of the ways to get over the problems. If a computer system has been properly designed and operated, then there should be almost no errors occurring.

Types of error

There are many different types of error. Some are easy to understand, others are very complicated. At GCSE level, we only need look at some of the simpler ones.

Errors in programming

If you write your own programs, you will come across many different types of **programming errors**. These are errors caused by careless typing or not thinking carefully enough about what you are doing. Examples might be:

1 **Syntax errors** – this is an error which occurs when the computer finds that something is wrong in the way you have written your program before it is even run. For example, in a BASIC program you may have carelessly written:

    100 RINT"Think of a number"
    instead of: 100 PRINT"Think of a number"

The interpreter or compiler (remember these terms?) does not recognize the keyword 'RINT', as this does not form part of the syntax of BASIC. **Syntax** is simply the 'set of rules' needed by BASIC so that your programs will be understood by the computer.

2 **Logical errors** – this type of error is when you have made a mistake in working out the logic of your program. The program will be properly interpreted or compiled, because all of the syntax is correct. An example of this type of error could be:

```
100 INPUT "Type in length of lawn in metres"; length
110 INPUT "Type in width of lawn in metres"; width
120 LET area = length + width
130 PRINT "The area of your lawn is"; area
140 PRINT "You will need"; area × 2/16 "pounds of seed"
```

In the above program, lines 100 and 110 ask the user to type in the length and width of their lawn. Line 120 is supposed to work out the area so that the weight of seeds needed can be worked out.

At line 120, the programmer should have got the computer to work out:

$$area = length \times width$$

So the programmer's maths is not that good!

The above program will run all right because there are no errors that the computer can detect. However, if it is used there will be many people going home with the wrong amount of seeds for their lawn. This is because the logic of the program is not correct.

There are many other programming errors such as making numbers too large for the computer to handle when doing its sums etc. (as when you make it divide 100 by zero). But this gives an idea of this type of error.

Errors in data entry

Sometimes, when we have written programs that work well, we still get errors due to people being careless when they are **entering** data. Although is it not possible to be 100 per cent correct, it is possible to reduce these errors to very small amounts.

As an example, let us suppose that we have developed a program to work out the average age of pupils in your class. Let us suppose that the ages range from 15 to 16 years. Now suppose that the following five ages are typed into the computer:

15·0, 15·2, 16·0, 15·8, 16·0

The computer would give you the correct answer of:

Average age in the class is 15.6

Now suppose that someone entered the data as follows:

15·0, 15·2, 16·0, 158, 16·0

If you look carefully you will see that the fourth age is now 158 instead of 15·8! That is they have forgotten the decimal point. However, the computer carries on and comes up with:

Average age in the class is 44.04

There are no mistakes in the program. The computer has not detected any errors but the answer is clearly a load of rubbish. This was human error in entering the data.

We will now look at some ways of reducing the above type of human error when data is being entered into the system:

Verification

One way of reducing the above type of error is to get two different people to type in the data. After the first person has typed in the data, it can be stored on a disc ready for the second person. When the second person types in the same data, it is compared with the first person's typing. Any difference between the two people's typing is then brought to the attention of the second person, who can check to see if the original data is wrong, or if they have made a mistake.

The process of checking to see if two sets of data are the same is called **verification**. The second person is verifying what the first person has done.

It must be realized that verification assumes that it is most unlikely that two different people will make exactly the same mistake when typing in the same set of data.

Validation

Verification would easily find the missing decimal point given in the age of your class example. But what about the following set of student ages?

15·0, 14·2, 16·0, 15·8, 16·0

They look all right. The computer gives an average age of 15·4 which sounds right. **But it is wrong**! If you look back to the beginning of the example, you will find that it said that the pupils in the class had ages between 15 and 16. In the above list we have a pupil who is 14·2. What should have been written down is 15·2. However, **both people involved in the verification check have correctly typed in the data that they have been given**.

What is needed is a further check **by the computer program** to see if the data being typed in is within a sensible **range**. In the above case we ought to check to see if the ages being typed in are between 15 and 16 inclusive. This sort of range check is called **validation**. It is a check to see if the **data is valid**. (It is acceptable.)

Besides checking for range, validation checks may also involve a check on the length of a string, or a check to see if numbers or letters are entered where they are expected. e.g. when entering dates etc.

Notice that we must still type in the data very carefully. No amount of checking by verification, validation or common sense would detect the following error:

15·0, 15·3, 16·0, 15·8, 16·0

15·3 has been written down instead of 15·2 for the second age. This type of error would get through all of the checks. The only way to get over this problem would be to get the computer to print out a list of names and

ages. You then ask the pupils if the age given is correct. You can rely on
the pupils to know their own age, can't you!

Summary

1 There are many different types of error. However, there are two major
types of errors called program errors and errors due to incorrect entry of
data.
2 Examples of program errors are errors in syntax and logical errors.
3 A syntax error is an error in the syntax (or grammar) of the program
(e.g. a misspelt keyword in BASIC).
4 A logical error is when the program has run properly, but has not
produced the expected output, because there is a mistake in the logic of
the program.
5 Human error when entering data can be reduced by verification and
validation.
6 Verification is when data is typed in twice by two different people. The
second set of data is compared with the first and any differences are
brought to the user's attention.
7 Validation is when the computer checks to see if the data being typed
in is sensible for the purpose (i.e. it is valid). A typical validation check
would be a check on the range of people's ages being fed into the
computer.

Revision questions

1 Give some reasons why errors occur in a computer system.
2 Give two examples of a program error.
3 What is a **syntax error**?
4 What is a logical error in a program?
5 What type of error would not be found during the compilation stage of
a program? (You will need to remember what a compiler is from
chapter 9. It is not mentioned in this chapter.)
6 How does verification reduce the possibility of human error when
entering data into a computer system?
7 What is the difference between verification and validation?
8 Explain how validation could work by using an example of typing in
some dates in the following form:

   16/12/86   31/2/87   1/2/45.

9 Even if a program is correct, and validation and verification have
been correctly carried out, it is still possible for minor errors to get
through the system. Give an example of this using the entry of dates.
10 An old lady receives an electricity bill for £1 000 000. If the program
allows such a ridiculous bill to get through the system, what does the
program need adding to it?

10 Data processing: large computers do this all day

Aims of this chapter

After reading through this chapter you should be able to:

K

1 Understand the term data processing (DP).
2 Understand a basic manual data processing system.
3 Compare manual data processing with computer data processing.
4 Understand some applications of data processing.

What is data processing?

K

Although computers are processing data all the time, the term **data processing** (DP) really belongs to the business world. Here large amounts of **data** must be **processed** so that information needed by the business can be got quickly and efficiently. Typical examples might be accounting, sales analysis, stock control, ordering and payroll applications.

In this chapter we look at some of the things which all the above processing applications (and many more) have in common.

Manual data processing

Many small businesses still use **manual** methods of processing data. Most people will be familiar with the necessary equipment. This would include filing cabinets, desks, input and output trays, calculators, files, folders, pencils and paper etc. That is, all the equipment that you would expect to find in a typical office.

Let's just think a little more carefully about the role of some of these, and the people who operate it. This will help us to compare the data processing system with the computer methods to be covered later in this chapter.

K

The system has an **input** (the in tray) and an **output** (the out tray). There are several types of **storage systems**. Very **short term store** may be notes written down on note paper; **long term store** would be permanent **records** which are kept in **files** inside the **filing cabinet**.

There is much processing that goes on. As an example, consider the following:

Suppose we are running a large second-hand car business with many branches. Let's assume that a customer has put in a request for a red Porsche.

The request must be picked up from the in tray. You would probably know whether or not you have a red Porsche in stock. But if your branch did not have it, you would have to go to the filing cabinet and get the lists of the other branches, to see if they have any in stock. If you can't find a Porsche on the list, you might phone round just in case a branch has got one which has not yet been put on the list. That is, you are going through a **search**. Also, even if a Porsche was on a list for another branch, you would still have to phone up to see if it had not been sold.

Suppose that you have found a suitable car. You must next contact the garage and get it delivered to your branch, or arrange for the customer to go to the other branch. This would involve sending information either by telephone or letter.

If the customer decides to buy the car, you will have to get all the necessary information from the **files**. You need to fill in information such as customer name and address, bank account number etc. on to several different forms and do many other routine processing jobs. That is, **a lot of data processing has to be done**.

After the sale has been confirmed, you would have to modify your **records** in the files so that the red Porsche is no longer available. You would have to notify the DVLC in Swansea about the change of ownership of the car. You would have to check that the money has been paid before giving the customer the car. You also would have to instruct the service department to give the Porsche the final 'once over'. That is, more processing of data is needed.

Computer techniques

Let us consider the same second-hand car example:

Instead of filing cabinets, desks, input and output trays, calculators, files, folders, pencils and paper etc. we are going to have a **computer system**. Our computer system would have **discs** (compare with the filing cabinet), **keyboard** (input), **printer** (output), **files**, a **VDU screen** and some other special hardware such as **modems** (see Chapter 15) so that the computer can communicate by telephone with computers at other branches.

We could easily get the computer to search for a red Porsche, first at our own branch, and then at the others (via the modem). The computer could quickly print out a list of the red Porsches that each branch has, together with the details of each car (e.g. age, mileage, condition etc). This list could be sent to the customer together with a standard letter obtained from the word processor. Or the customer could be phoned up and given the information. That is, the **computer is doing a lot of the data processing**.

When a computer is used for data processing, it is often called **electronic data processing** or **EDP** for short. The important thing to realize is that there is really little difference in principle between what is going on in the computer and manual systems. It is just the techniques and equipment that are different. Of course the computer is a lot faster, and takes a lot of the hard and boring work away from the sales people. They can then concentrate on keeping the customers happy!

An application of computer data processing

We will now look at the second-hand car dealer network application in a little more detail:

It is important to look at the whole system when considering data processing. For example,

1 How does the data for new cars get entered into the system?
2 What checking should there be for data entry?
3 How will the computers at the different branches communicate with each other?
4 What files will be necessary?
5 Who will operate the system?
6 What type of backing store is needed?
7 What type of programs must be written?
8 Is there a commercial system available that will do the job?
9 Is the system really necessary?
10 What form should the output from the computer take?

The above are just a few of the hundreds of possible questions that need to be asked and answered, when a large data processing application may be set up. Perhaps question **9** is one of the most important? Some of the above questions will now be answered.

Is the system really necessary?
If you had to write down some of the reasons why you want an EDP system then they might be as follows:

1 To speed up the customer enquiry service, especially if a customer is waiting.
2 To improve the accuracy of the information given to the customer, for example a computer printout of all details from other branches instead of many hasty telephone calls.
3 To improve the quality of the service. For example, while the computer is doing all the inquiring, you can be having a nice glass of champagne with the customer explaining that the computer system is finding their ideal car. Also, the computer can quickly match such requests as age, mileage, condition and price etc.

Having convinced ourselves that the service would be much better with the aid of a computerized data processing system, let's have a look at some possible methods we could use.

The storage needed
This would obviously be discs as an enquiry must be dealt with while a customer is waiting. The size of the discs needed would depend upon the amount of information that needs to be stored. This in turn will depend on the size of the business and the number of cars in stock. A Winchester disc would probably be used at each branch in this application.
Is there a head office? If so, does head office want to or need to store information about the cars in all its branches? If this is the case, then each computer in the local salesrooms would only need to search the computer at head office to get any information about cars in all other branches. A typical diagram for a local branch is shown in Fig. 1.

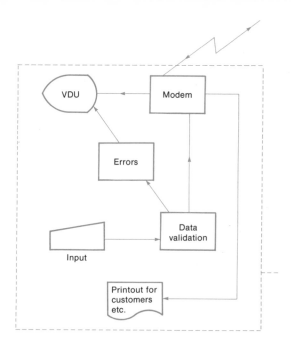

Fig. 1

It would be sensible to store all the information at head office. Therefore, head office would need a larger and more expensive computer and storage system.

How is data entered into the system?
When a car is bought by the business it could be from an auction or taken in part exchange for another car. Much information has therefore to be processed during these transactions.

There will be a registration document with each car. Details from this will need to be typed into the computer system by using a keyboard and a VDU. If the system is to be convenient to use, then a proper screen display will need to be developed. One way would be to use a mouse to point to a box on the screen where data is to be entered. After typing in the data, you click the mouse to confirm that the data input is finished. The computer will then validate the data if possible. The mouse is then moved to the next box and the process repeated.

What files will be needed?
File design is very important but has been covered in other chapters. However, you can easily estimate how large the file will be by finding out the average number of characters that are needed to describe a car. Then multiply by the maximum number of cars that you think it is likely that the data processing system will ever have to cope with. When you have done this, you also allow a little more!

What data processing will be carried out?
Will the system just be used for storing information about the stock of cars, or will it be extended to cope with other things such as word processing, or even working out the wages of the employees? What about working out sales commission, profits, statistics about which cars sell best etc.?

Once you have an electronic data processing system, the ways of extending its use are enormous. Electronic mail between the different branches is an obvious example in this case. Why pay postage to send letters when you have a computer system connected to each branch, which can send messages instantaneously?

One of the silly errors that people make is realizing the potential of a system **after** it has been installed and then expecting the system to cope with things for which it was not designed. The systems analysis chapter explains how these problems should be overcome. Here it is enough to explain the sort of data processing that can be carried out by computer. A typical list is as follows:

Typical data processing activities

Sorting – sorting lists into a certain order (e.g. alphabetical or numerical). In our car sales example this could be an alphabetical list of cars together with price, for putting into an advertisement in the local newspaper.

Searching – finding a particular item or items of interest. This is used when a customer makes a specific request (e.g. a **blue car** which has done **less than 10 000 miles** that costs **less than £5000** but **has four doors**).

Classifying – making lists of useful **statistics** such as the make of car that sells most, the types of cars on which most profit is made, or types of cars that do not sell well. With such information, management can decide how much to charge for each type of car.

Printed lists and **reports** – in our car sales system, these could be lists of customers. For example, Christmas cards may be automatically addressed and sent. Also, monthly reports on the financial or stock situation for the board of directors.

Storing – getting the system to store information conveniently so that it may be recalled very quickly.

Arithmetic – getting the system to work out things like profit etc. automatically by using the information that is stored in the standard records for each car (e.g. buying price and selling price).

The above is not intended to be a complete system. It is simply to make you realize what advantages can be had by using an electronic data processing system instead of a manual one.

Summary

1 Data processing is the general term for computers used to help with getting information processed, so that a business can quickly, accurately and efficiently find and use this information.
2 Data processing can be manual (e.g. the use of filing cabinets, paper, calculators and other standard office equipment).
3 Electronic data processing (EDP or simply DP) is the replacement of some or all of the manual system by computer.
4 There are many similarities between electronic data processing and manual data processing (e.g. you can identify input, output, storage and processing in each system).
5 If a data processing system is installed, then it is important to realize the full uses to which the system can be put. Systems analysis covered in Chapter 16 will explain how people go about getting the most out of any proposed system.
6 Typical data processing activities include searching, sorting, storing, filing, classifying, printing reports and lists, doing arithmetic and many other similar operations.

Revision questions

1 What is **data processing**?
2 Do you need a computer to carry out data processing?
3 What is **electronic data processing**?
4 Give some typical examples of data processing.
5 Give a typical example of some of the equipment that would be needed when manual data processing is carried out.
6 List four different reasons why a computer might be used instead of a manual data processing system.
7 Data processing can be thought of as a system being made up of processes such as sorting, storing, filing etc. List three other common DP operations.
8 What sort of things do you have to take into consideration when thinking of what type of storage would be necessary in a data processing system?
9 What is meant by **printed reports** when applied to a DP system?
10 What could happen if unvalidated data entered the system? (Hint: you will need to look at Chapter 10 if you can't remember what validation means.)

11 Representing data: have a BYTE of this BIT!

Aims of this chapter

After reading through this chapter you should be able to:

K
1 Understand what is meant by binary, and why binary is used.
2 Represent characters in simple ways.
3 Understand binary pulse trains.
4 Understand and be able to use even and odd parity.

Why binary is used. Computer chit chat

If you overheard two computers talking to each other about the decimal system it might go something like this:
  'I don't know why humans count in base ten, I think it must be something to do with the fact that they have ten fingers.' 'It seems a most unnatural way of counting.'

K
  We only think of base ten (decimal or denary) as natural because we have used it since childhood. For computers, **binary** or **base two** is a more natural way. This is because it is easy to detect if electricity is switched on or off. This leads to a system of numbers using just two symbols: 0 and 1. First, a quick reminder of counting in binary:
  The following table shows the columns for counting in binary and base ten. We have counted up to 20 in each system.

Base Ten	Base Two	Base Ten	Base Two
0	0	11	1011
1	01	12	1100
2	10	13	1101
3	11	14	1110
4	100	15	1111
5	101	16	10000
6	110	17	10001
7	111	18	10010
8	1000	19	10011
9	1001	20	10100
10	1010		

Remember the column headings in base two? These are 8s, 4s, 2s, 1s etc. That is, times by two to get from one column to the next column.
  In this way, we can easily work out that 10110 (base two) is 22 (base ten). Simply write down the number under the appropriate column headings as follows:

Column headings	16	8	4	2	1
Binary number	1	0	1	1	0

1 lot of 16 and 1 lot of 4 and 1 lot of 2 is 22 (base ten).

How computers use binary to represent data

If computers use binary, how on earth can they work with text? For example, how are all the characters used by a word processor dealt with?

Very early on, it was realized that if people were to share data on different computers then some sort of **code** would be necessary. If everybody agreed on the same code, then different computers could work together. Life was not quite that simple, there were several codes that acted as a 'standard'. However, we will look at one of the most popular called **ASCII**. This stands for **American Standard Code for Information Interchange**.

Part of the ASCII code for the letters A to D is shown in the following table:

Character	Decimal code	Binary code
A	65	1 0 0 0 0 0 1
B	66	1 0 0 0 0 1 0
C	67	1 0 0 0 0 1 1
D	68	1 0 0 0 1 0 0

What is binary for character 'E'?

(You should have been able to work out the binary column! For example, A has a binary code of 1 0 0 0 0 0 1 because we need 1 lot of 64 and 1 lot of 1.) Were you right? E is 1 0 0 0 1 0 1. To save you working out each code, you can get your computer to print them out for you. In some versions of BASIC, this would be as follows:

PRINT ASC("A") would cause 65 to be printed on the screen. Try it if you can. Replace "A" with "W", and the ASCII code for W should be printed. Also, try PRINT CHR$(65) to print "A".

Suppose we were to peep inside some memory locations, and suppose that we came across the word 'CAB'. The binary patterns to represent these words using the above system would be:

C	1 0 0 0 0 1 1
A	1 0 0 0 0 0 1
B	1 0 0 0 0 1 0

Each binary digit (that is, 0 or 1) is called a **bit**. (Short for **B**inary dig**IT**). The BIT is the smallest unit of data that could be stored inside a computer.

Many computers, (especially micros) work in groups of eight bits. Also, many of the memory chips store eight bits at once. Each group of eight bits has therefore been given a name. They are called a **byte**. Increasingly, micros are becoming 16-bit, which can store two 8-bit codes, and even 32-bit, which can store four 8-bit codes.

If we had a memory chip that stored every character as an eight-bit byte, then the three letters CAB would be stored as:

C	0 1 0 0 0 0 1 1
A	0 1 0 0 0 0 0 1
B	0 1 0 0 0 0 1 0

Binary pulse trains

Sometimes it is necesssary to send characters **serially** (one after the other) down a single wire. The telephone is a good example of this. The same types of ASCII code can still be used but this time we have to send each bit one after the other. We can send a binary **one** by sending a single **pulse** down the wire. A binary **zero** can be **no pulse**. We can see the idea for sending the character 'A' as follows:

ASCII code   0   1   0   0   0   0   0   1
Pulse train

The **binary pulse train** for 'C' would be:

ASCII code   0   1   0   0   0   0   1   1
Pulse train

In practice, these pulse trains would be sent very quickly, many thousands each second. Also, you have to know where they start and stop, or you could get very confused.

Parity. Making sure it's right

There are ways to check to see if the messages you receive are likely to be the ones that were sent. This is necessary because sometimes the electrical signals can be messed up by interference. A very simple check is called a **parity check**. This involves counting up the number of ones in the binary number. As an example, consider the following:

Characters	ASCII codes	Binary pattern (eight-bits)	No of 1s
H	72	0 1 0 0 1 0 0 0	2 (even)
E	69	0 1 0 0 0 1 0 1	3 (odd)
L	76	0 1 0 0 1 1 0 0	3 (odd)
L	76	0 1 0 0 1 1 0 0	3 (odd)
O	79	0 1 0 0 1 1 1 1	5 (odd)

Notice that the first digit for each byte is zero. This digit is not used for the letter codes and can therefore be used for parity.

If we make sure that there are an even number of ones in each byte then it is called **even parity**.

Even parity for the word 'HELLO' is shown in the following table:

Characters	ASCII codes	Even parity
H	72	0 1 0 0 1 0 0 0
E	69	1 1 0 0 0 1 0 1
L	76	1 1 0 0 1 1 0 0
L	76	1 1 0 0 1 1 0 0
O	79	1 1 0 0 1 1 1 1

Parity bit ⌐

Notice that when parity is used, the parity bit is needed to make an even number of ones when necessary.

The way that the system operates is that when the character is transmitted the parity bit is added and transmitted with it as shown above. A check is then performed on the received data by counting up the number of ones, including the parity bit. If it is not even then an error has been detected.

Some systems use **odd parity** which works in the same way except that an odd number of ones are used.

Summary

1 Binary is the name for numbers in base two.
2 Computers naturally use binary because it is easiest to detect if electricity is on or off (i.e. two states).
3 Characters (numbers and letters etc.) are represented inside the computer as binary codes. ASCII is a good example.
4 ASCII stands for American Standard Code for Information Interchange.
5 A binary pulse train is a train of serial pulses for sending characters one after the other.
6 Parity is a method of checking to see if the received data contains any errors.

Revision questions

1 What is a **binary number**?
2 Convert 1001 (base two) into a number in base ten.
3 What is a **bit**?
4 What is a **byte**? Why are bytes used?
5 How can characters be represented inside a computer?
6 What do the letters ASCII stand for?
7 What is the ASCII code for 'B'?
8 What is meant by **parity**?
9 Does the following message use odd or even parity?

ASCII	Decimal	Bytes sent	
G	71	0 1 0 0 1 0 0 0	
O	79	1 1 0 0 1 1 1 1	
O	79	1 1 0 0 1 1 1 1	
D	68	0 1 0 0 0 1 0 0	
	32	1 0 1 0 0 0 0 0 ←—	(this is the
B	66	0 1 0 0 0 0 1 0	code for
Y	89	1 1 0 1 1 0 0 1	space)
E	69	1 1 0 0 0 1 0 1	

10 There is an error in the binary digit table in question **9**. Can you use parity to check which one it is? What should have been sent?

12 Fields and files

Aims of the chapter

After reading through this chapter you should be able to:

1 Understand what a file is.
2 Understand the terms record, field and character.
3 Explain what is meant by a key field, and why it is important.
4 Know what is meant by a master and transaction file.
5 Understand the terms updating, merging, sorting and searching.
6 Understand the use of grandfather, father and son files.
7 Understand the need for file security.

What is a file?

There is nothing special or difficult to understand about a file. It means exactly the same thing as the file in a filing cabinet at home or in the office. For example, you or your parents may have a file in which the monthly bank statements are kept. If you want to find out information such as 'has a cheque been paid', or 'how much money did you have in the bank on a certain day', you can get this information from the file.

If your bank file is well organized, you should be able to find such information quickly by searching through the papers in the file.

The idea of a file in computing is similar to that described above. A **file** is simply **a collection of related information**. Instead of being stored on pieces of paper in a filing cabinet, computer files are stored in special ways on disc or tape.

You have to be well organized!

If you don't keep a manual filing system tidy you will find it difficult to find information. Computer files must also be very well organized, or the computer will not be able to find the correct item of information.

Just like the manual system, a computer file is split up into **records**. For example, the first six records for a second-hand car dealer might be as shown in Fig. 1.

Fig. 1

| Make & model | Registration number | Colour | c.c. | Mileage | Condition | Make & |

The information about each car can be found in the record belonging to that car. Each **record** is split up into several **fields**. In our car sales file, these fields are make and model, registration number, colour, cubic capacity (c.c.), mileage and condition. We can see that each record has six fields. Finally, each **field** can hold a certain number of **characters**. For example, the registration number field can have a maximum of seven characters.

When using computer files, the length of each field is very important. If it is too long, then space can be wasted when the information is stored.

If it is too short, then some important information may not be able to fit. A happy medium must be arrived at. Most of the usual information must fit in. Anything unusual may have to be shortened.

As an example, how many characters do you think ought to be chosen for a surname? 10 or 15? 20 or 30? How about looking in a telephone directory? 12 may seem reasonable. However, it will not be able to store surnames like 'Cohen-Tonnoudji'. This might have to be shortened to Cohen-T or some other suitable name to which the owner does not object too much!

The key field

Each record is usually identified by a **key field**. This is the field containing the information by which the record is known. For example, if there was a Rolls Royce Silver Shadow in stock, then this would be the information contained in the key field. It would identify the Rolls Royce Silver Shadow's record. Other fields in this record would contain information about registration number, colour etc. for this Silver Shadow.

When a computer searches through a file, it uses the key field to identify a particular record. For example, if you asked for a Rover 2000, then all the records for Rover 2000 cars may be printed out.

Often, it is best to have a **unique key field**. For example, a bank may have customers with the same surname and initials. It would be embarrassing if information about one customer were wrongly sent to another. In this case, and many other similar situations, it is usual to have a unique customer number as the key field (e.g. your bank account number).

Master and transaction files

All the files used on computers can be given a name depending on their use. The way that information is stored inside them is not necessarily different. It is simply a label given to a file used for a certain job.

For example, a file that contains up-to-date information, and one that is often used to answer queries is called a **master file**. Typical examples of master files might be:

1 The levels of stock in a supermarket.
2 The names and addresses of people in a football club.

and many many others.

Imagine that you are the manager of a large commercial retail chain of shops. Your company has a minicomputer at head office containing the master files which have all the information about your business. Let's just concentrate on the sales master file.

Whenever you sell something to a customer, the posh name for this process is called a **transaction**. At the end of the day, information about sales from your branches reaches head office. That is, the information about all the transactions reaches head office.

All this information is entered into the computer system and sorted into some convenient order. The file that contains information about the day's sales is therefore called the **transaction file**.

When the transaction file is ready, it can then be used to update the master file automatically. After this computer run, the master file will contain the latest information about the businesses. The exact amount of stock is then known, and reordering might be carried out if necessary.

There are many situations where the transaction files are used to update the master files. It does not have to happen daily as in the above example, it might be weekly, monthly, or even quarterly. Also, we do not **have** to have a transaction file to produce a master file. For example, a file of boys in the school, together with a file of girls in the school could be used to produce a master file of pupils in the school.

File processing

Updating – Keeping it up to date!

No file will be of any use unless it contains the most up-to-date information. **Updating** is therefore a process that is frequently carried out. Keeping files up to date is also known as maintaining the files or simply **file maintenance**. However, we have to be very careful about how we update the information on a computer. Get it wrong, and you might not be able to get the correct information back again! Some ways of making sure that updating is carried out properly are covered later in the chapter.

Sorting

This is the process of **sorting** a file into a certain order. This might be alphabetical order or customer number order, to name but two. When files are sorted, it is usually by using the key field (remember what this is?). All the other information in the record (another term you should know) goes with the key field when this sorting process takes place.

If information is sorted into some sensible order, it is easier for the computer to find what it is looking for. The process of sorting is so common that many commercial programs (packages) exist simply to sort things into alphabetical or numerical (number) order.

Merging

Merging is a simple process of joining two or more files together to make one. The idea is shown in Fig. 2. Tape has been used in this example, but files can also be merged on disc.

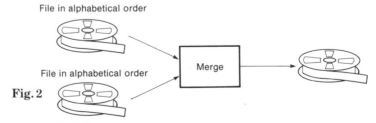

File in alphabetical order

File in alphabetical order

Merge

Fig. 2

Earlier we saw how a transaction file can be used to update a master file. One way of carrying out this process is to start by sorting the transaction file into alphabetical order. Next, assuming that the master file is also in alphabetical order, the master file and transaction file can be merged to produce the **new master file**.

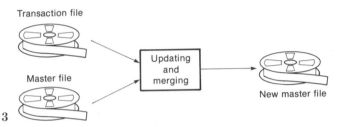

Fig. 3

Searching
Searching means looking through a file until you find the record of interest. With tape systems searching is a slow process. Each record would have to be looked at to see if it was the one that was required. If not, the next record would be looked at. The process would continue until the correct record was found. This sort of process, where each record before the one that you want has to be looked at, is called **serial access**. If the records are sorted into order, then this is known as **sequential access**.
A much quicker method is called **random access**. This is a method where it is possible to get to a record without having to read all the previous records. It is not possible to use random access on tape. With this faster method, discs must be used.
When dealing with thousands of records it is possible to find the record of interest in a few fractions of a second on disc using random access methods. Such methods would therefore be ideal for files dealing with booking tickets for airlines etc. where a quick response is important.
We must not dismiss serial access using tape. This is a common method and is often used when it is not necessary to find a single record, but only necessary to process thousands of records one after the other (i.e. serially). Examples where this is the most efficient way are files containing quarterly payments such as gas and electricity bills or rates etc. where once every 3 months it is usual to process a batch of bills. This process is known as **batch processing**.

Grandfather, father and son files: keeping it in the family!

Earlier we saw that updating is an important process when using computer files. We will now describe a simple method which is used to make sure that you have a good chance to recover from mistakes that may be made, or files that get lost or damaged. The process can be explained by looking at Fig. 4.
In the beginning, the original master file, called the **FATHER FILE**,

is used with the **TRANSACTION FILE** to produce a new master file called the **son**.

Some time later, when the next transaction file is ready, the same process is repeated. That is, the latest master file is used with the latest transaction file to produce a **third-generation master file** which is called the **son**. The second-generation master file is now called the **father**, and finally the original master file is called the **grandfather**.

What happens next time round? It would be silly to keep on going producing great-grandfathers etc. Therefore it has been decided that three generations of files are enough to give a very good chance of recovering from any errors that might be made. Next time round the original master file is no longer kept. In practice, this does not mean that it is physically thrown away, but simply wiped clean or used for the latest son file.

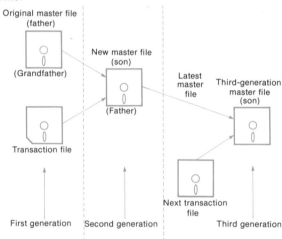

Fig. 4

There are two important things to consider. First there is the **physical security** of files (i.e. keeping them safe from being stolen, being destroyed by fire or magnetic fields etc.). Second there is the **security necessary to prevent people from getting information from the computer system illegally** (e.g. looking at other people's bank accounts or other companies' secret plans etc.).

The first of these security problems is relatively easy to deal with. To keep data safe from fire, backup copies are stored in a different building. Fireproof data storage boxes are also a possibility.

Another, perhaps more likely event, is that someone accidently erases that data by doing something silly with the system. Backup copies again come in handy. Also, it is often possible with data that does not change to put a write protect mechanism on magnetic tape or disc. This will ensure that data can only be read from the disc or tape (i.e. data can't be wiped off).

Security of data from unauthorized access is much more complicated. You can never be absolutely sure that data is secure as most breaches of security are an inside job.

One way to protect data from casual observers is to have a system of **passwords**. On some systems, different passwords can give you different levels of access. For example one type of password may allow the user only to look at the data. A more important user may have to use a different password to allow them to both look at and change the data on the files.

Security is now more important than ever, especially with the advent of computer networks where confidential information is transmitted over the telephone line.

Summary

1 A file is a collection of related information.

2 Many records usually make up a file. A record contains information about one particular part of the file, (e.g. a record for each person who is a member of a club).

3 Records are split up into fields. Each field usually contains just a single item of data (e.g. the name or address field in a record).

4 A character is simply a letter, number or special symbol such as £, %, etc. One or more characters make up a field.

5 A key field is the field which is used to identify a particular record. In most cases, the key field is unique, as with customer identity number.

6 Files are given special names according to their uses. Master files contain the latest information, and are frequently used for reference. Transaction files contain the latest transactions and are used to update the master file periodically.

7 Updating, or file maintenance, is the process of keeping files up to date.

8 Merging is the name given to the process where two files are used to create one file. A typical example of merging is when the transaction file and old master file are used to create a new master file.

9 Sorting is the name given to arranging the key fields into some order such as alphabetical or customer number etc.

10 Searching is the name given to the process of finding a record within a particular file. If all the previous records have to be searched through it is called serial access. If the records are sorted into order then it is called sequential access. However, if you can go to the item of interest without having to read all other items before it, it is called random access, and is only possible with discs.

11 Three generations of files used to ensure a fair degree of security to recover from errors. These are called grandfather, father and son files.

12 File security can be split into two parts:

(a) The physical security of files such as protection against theft or fire, accidental erasure etc.
(b) The protection of the data from unauthorized entry. Passwords are often used to achieve this.

Revision questions

1 What is meant by a **file**?
2 How is a computer file organized? Give an example showing clearly how it is split up into records, fields and characters.
3 Why is the key field important to files?
4 What is the difference between a master and transaction file?
5 Show, by means of a diagram, how a master file and a transaction file could be used to produce the latest master file.
6 What is meant by **file maintenance**? Why is this important?
7 Why do you think it is necessary for the master file and transaction file in question **5** to be sorted?
8 What is meant by the term **merging**?
9 Why is a random access search much quicker that a serial access search?
10 Why is sequential access ideal for batch processing?
11 Would serial access or random access be ideal for airline enquiries?
12 How would you prevent accidental erasure of data from a disc or tape?
13 You discover that yesterday's master file has been accidentally erased. What can you do about it?
14 Name one system of protecting data from unauthorized access by people using a computer system.

13 Low level languages: definitely not English!

Aims of this chapter

After reading through this chapter you should be able to:

1 Understand what is meant by a low level language, and why low level languages are needed.
2 Recognize some simple low level language type instructions.
3 Understand why assemblers are needed.

What is a low level language?

Can you remember what basic units make up a computer system? They are input, output, the CPU (central processing unit) and storage. We are now going to have a brief look at how the computers can use these basic units to perform all the wonderful things that computers can do.

Think for a moment about several different computer uses, for example word processing, payroll, stock control or even computer games. All these things are being done by a computer system that is made up from the same basic units of input, output, CPU and storage.

How can these same pieces of hardware do all of these different things? The answer is obviously software. But how does the software control the hardware? If you type in a BASIC high level language instruction like:

100 PRINT"The cat sat on the mat."

When the program is RUN, you would expect the characters 'The cat sat on the mat.' to appear on the computer screen. But how is it actually done? Something somewhere must organize the insides of the computer. We know that the computer works using binary numbers like 01100110 and 10010011. The binary pattern makes the electricity inside the machine go along a particular path which causes the right things to happen. But how does the above program line get changed into this form?

I think you would agree from the above that a lot of complicated things need to be done. What actually goes on inside the machine is very different from the commands given to the computer in a high level language. The high level language was designed to make the computer easy to use.

We must therefore have some other language which is much closer to what actually goes on inside the machine. This is called a **low level language**.

Let's have a look at all this low level language stuff

Firstly, because we are controlling what goes on inside the computer, we need to look at the CPU in a little more detail.

The inside of the CPU is very complex, but we can get a good idea of the main parts, and how a low level language can be used to control them.

A simple CPU consists of an **accumulator** (a temporary store), an **arithmetic unit** (place where the sums are done), and a **control unit** (a unit which controls the entire operation of the system). The idea is shown in Fig. 1.

The figure also shows an **electronic clock**. This provides a tick-tock, tick-tock type rhythm which keeps all the electronic circuits in time with each other. You can imagine that it is similar to a little man conducting an orchestra. However, inside the computer he would be waving his arms up and down several million times a second!

If we keep with the idea of music for a moment, you can imagine the

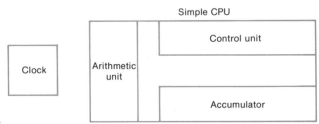

Fig. 1

conductor conducting music which has three beats to the bar. Inside the computer, however, this 'music' would be very boring, and the three beats would be fetch – decode – execute, fetch – decode – execute, fetch – decode – execute over and over again. But what is this strange 'music'?

This **fetch – decode – execute cycle** means that an **instruction** in a **low level language** is **fetched** from store, **decoded** (to see what the instruction is asking the computer to do), and then **executed** (the instruction is carried out).

Once you have appreciated the above, you are well on the way to understanding in simple terms how the insides of computers work. **They are going through this fetch – decode – execute cycle all the time**. Even if you have just switched the computer on, there may be a program inside that is waiting so see if a key on the keyboard has been pressed. That is, the computer is going through the fetch – decode – execute cycle.

The next question is, what is being fetched, decoded and executed? The answer is **low level language instructions**. Some simple ones for one type of computer may be:

LOAD #27
ADD #28
STORE (21)

This could be a program to ADD the number 27 to 28, and then STORE the answer in memory location 21. These very simple operations are typical of what has to be done in a low level language.

You will remember that computers work in binary. Each simple instruction such as ADD, STORE etc. will have been given a special code.

For example, LOAD   might be   00101010
       ADD   might be   00100011
       STORE might be   00100100

Not forgetting that the numbers 27, 28 and 21 will need a code, if we looked inside the computer you may see the program represented by the following code:

00101010 00011011	Which is the	LOAD	27
00100011 00011100	code for . . .	ADD	28
00100100 00010101		STORE	(21)

You will agree that the code on the left is awkward to work with. It is just a mass of 0s and 1s. This is what the machine has to work with and it is called **machine code**.

When people have to write programs in a low level language, it is not convenient to use lots of 0s and 1s. Mistakes are too easily made. It is far better to use the simpler instructions shown above on the right. This uses **mnemonics** (an aid to the memory) and is called **assembly language**. The mnemonics uses groups of letters to jog the memory as to what it means. So **LDA** might be **LoaD** the Accumulator and **STA** might be **STore** the Accumulator. However, when assembly language is being used, you have to get the computer to convert all of the mnemonics into the machine code that will eventually be used.

How does this link up with fetch – decode – execute?

When you have written a program on a computer it must be stored somewhere inside the computer's memory. Let's assume that our little program shown above lives in three memory locations as follows:

Address   1000   00101010   00011011
Address   1001   00100011   00011100
Address   1002   00100100   00010101

Each memory location in the computer will have its own **address**. There will usually be thousands of these but we have only shown three.

When the computer runs the program it will start off by **fetching** the instruction at memory location 1000.

The control unit will then **decode** 00101010 00011011 to find out that this means:

LOAD # 27

It will then **execute** this command. That is, number 27 will be placed inside the accumulator (remember the temporary store in the CPU) ready to be used in the next operation.

The next two instructions are fetched, decoded and executed in a similar way. The answer to the sum will be found in memory location 21. The arithmetic unit actually worked out the answer to the sum.

All of that to add two numbers . . . you must be joking!

If you think that the above was a ridiculous amount of work just to add two simple numbers together, then you are starting to appreciate what writing programs in assembly language or machine code is like (i.e. very tedious and difficult).

Compare this with a high level language instruction to do the same sort of thing:

10 PRINT 27+28

The answer will even appear on the screen automatically for you!

However, **all instructions in a high level language must be translated into instructions in a low level language to work on the computer**. It is just fortunate that you do not have to write all the complicated low level language programs to do this.

Just think of the above in terms of driving a car. Most people can do that very easily. However, it is fortunate that we do not have to understand the turbo charger or the fuel injection unit to drive the car. Someone else has done all this hard work for us. Just as you should appreciate that the car has an engine, gearbox, clutch etc. you should appeciate that all high level languages on the computer must be changed into low level languages before they can be used.

Assemblers

We have seen that it is tedious to write programs in machine code. We have also seen that it is easier to write programs using the simpler instructions such as LOAD # 27 etc. We should also know by now that, in the end, nothing inside computers happens without being turned into machine code. So we need a program that **translates** these simpler instructions into machine code. The program that performs this translation is called an **assembler**, and the instructions such as LOAD # 27 are called **assembly language instructions**.

It is far easier to program in assembly language than to use the awkward binary machine code instructions. It is also far easier to change assembly language into machine code than it is a high level language like BASIC.

As well as converting the code for you, assemblers will also do many other useful things such as listing your assembly language programs. It also provides tables of numbers to help the programmer and some help with finding errors in the programs.

Summary

1 Low level languages are languages that reflect what is actually going on inside the machine.

2 It is much harder to program in a low level language than the easy-to-use high level languages.

3 The binary code (1s and 0s) that is used inside the computer to represent the program is called machine code.

4 Machine code is difficult to use as it consists of only 1s and 0s.

5 Assembly languages are much easier to use than machine code as a few mnemonics (aids to the memory) are used instead of 1s and 0s.

6 Both machine code and assembly language are examples of low level languages.

7 A simple CPU consists of an accumulator (temporary store), an arithmetic unit (place where the sums are done) and a control unit (a device which controls the entire operation). The whole process is controlled by an electronic clock.

8 Programs are stored inside the computer's memory as low level language instructions. Each instruction has to be fetched from memory,

decoded by the control unit and then executed (i.e. the correct action taken).
9 An assembler translates the assembly language instructions into machine code that will run on the computer.
10 Assembly language is a low level language program, written using instructions like LOAD # 27, STORE (35) etc. These are instructions to aid the memory and are called mnemonics.

Revision questions

1 Give an advantage of a high level over a low level language.
2 What is **machine code**?
3 Why is it rare to program in machine code?
4 What is a **mnemonic**?
5 Why is assembly language easier to use than machine code?
6 **What is an accumulator**?
7 Why do computers need an electronic clock?
8 What is meant by the term **translation**?
9 What is an **assembly language**?
10 What does an assembler do?

14 Operating systems: I'm in charge!

Aims of this chapter

After reading through this chapter you should be able to:

1 Understand why operating systems are needed.
2 Understand the following types of operating system:
(a) batch; (b) on-line; (c) network; (d) real time.
3 Know some simple functions of the operating system.
4 Understand and give some examples of utilities and applications programs.

Why are operating systems needed?

If you have read Chapter 13, then you will appreciate that it is very tedious and difficult to program the computer to do even the most simple tasks. For example:

1 Getting a character from the keyboard.

2 Writing some data to the disc drive.
3 Making sure that the computer does not send characters to the printer too quickly etc.

are all examples of things that we take for granted. However, we should now know that nothing inside the computer happens without someone telling the computer what to do by means of a program. There are many programs inside the computer that carry out all the tasks described above, and also many more. This **suite** (or collection) of programs is called the **operating system**.

It is just as well that the makers of computers supply an operating system, because without it the computer would be almost impossible to use. You would certainly have to be a computer expert to do even the most simple operation. So the operating system is the programs that make the computer easy to use by nonspecialists. They make the computer **user friendly**. In fact some computer operating systems are so user friendly that complete beginners can now use computers quite easily. A good example of this is the GEM operating system. **GEM** stands for **G**raphics **E**nvironment **M**anager. In this you use **icons** which are little pictures. A mouse can be used to point to the **dustbin icon**, for example, to get rid of some work (see Fig. 1).

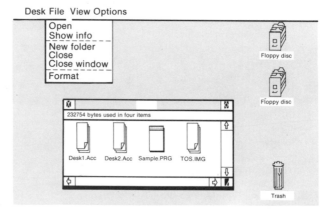

Fig. 1

Different types of operating systems
Operating systems control the operation of a computer. They make the hardware easy to use. We should not be surprised to see more complicated operating systems on more expensive computer systems.

Each operating system belongs to a group depending on the jobs which it can do. For example, if a simple computer can only have one user at a time, then it is referred to as a **single-user operating system**. Similarly, if many users can use the system at any one time, then it would be referred to as a **multi-user operating system**. We will now look at some of the main types.

Types of operating systems

1 *Batch operating systems*
This is an operating system where a **batch** of jobs (a set of programs to be run) can be put into the computer system and run one after the other. It is one method of providing large computers with many things to do, so that the computer is not idle.

Often much processing has to be done in a batch. For example, doing the gas or rates accounts for thousands of people at the same time. Such methods are ideal when the data is stored sequentially (remember this term?) on tape. This type of processing is called **batch processing**.

2 *On-line operating systems*
When dealing with **batch operating systems** mentioned above, it is possible for the job to be given to the computer system and run several hours (or even days) later. This does not really matter when processing gas and rates bills etc. (In fact the author often wishes that it would take years to send out the bills!) However, this delay would not be acceptable if you were waiting for the results of a program. Imagine typing in an instruction to the computer system and getting the result 2 days later!

A different type of operating system is therefore needed – one that will respond very quickly to any input from the users. As you have to be connected to the system for this to happen, it is called an **on-line** operating system. Compare this with batch, where you submit the job to the computer system and see the results at some late time. You do not have to be connected to the computer system when the job is run. Batch operating systems are therefore **off-line**.

If you are used to using a microcomputer then some of these terms may seem a little strange. However, if you think of them as large computers doing many different things for different users, the terms make more sense.

3 *Network operating systems*
Networks are computers connected together, so that they can all share expensive resources that would otherwise have to be duplicated. For example, if 26 pupils in a class each have their own disc drive and printer this would prove to be very expensive. Another main reason for a network is so that every computer can share the information from the main database.

An alternative to the above is to connect the computers together to form a network of computers. Each computer would be able to share a single disc drive and printer. If the disc drive is a Winchester (you should know what that is!) then the results are often quicker than if each pupil had their own floppy disc drive.

Obviously the software to control this system is much more complicated than the software needed to control the micros individually. This special suite of programs would be called a **network operating system**.

The other major advantage of a network operating system is that all the computers connected to the network can communicate with each other. Such systems are ideal for electronic mail facilities, etc.

4 *Real time systems*
With most operating systems, it does not matter if you have to wait half a second for the results you are expecting. Indeed, on most systems you would not even notice any delay.

Sometimes, even a fraction of a second delay could be fatal. For example, suppose a computer system is used to fire and guide a missile that is going to intercept another missile that has been fired at you!

When using computers for military defence purposes such as that mentioned above, we have to have the fastest possible response that we are able to get. The efficiency of using the computer system is no longer important (i.e. the computer does not have to get the most amount of work done that it is possible to do). All that is necessary is that there is a massive amount of computing power ready the instant that it is needed.

Systems like those described above have to respond instantly to an emergency situation. They are called **real time systems** and the operating systems that control them are called **real time operating systems**.

The operating system . . .is that all we get?

When you buy a computer system, the operating system is part of the basic package. On small computers it is usually in ROM, but on larger computers it is usually on disc. We have seen how the operating system takes care of all the basic things that we take for granted, such as sending characters to the printer etc. However, even with all these basic things taken care of, there are still many things which most users would like to be able to do. For example:

1 Copying one disc to another (i.e. making a backup).
2 Cataloguing the contents of a disc.
3 Formatting a disc (making it ready for storing data).
4 Sorting lists into alphabetical order etc.

All the above facilities and many more are often included with the computer system. They are lots of useful special-purpose programs called **utilities**. If the utility is specially for a disc, such as a formatter, then it is called a **disc utility**.

Applications programs

Finally, the computer would still be inconvenient to use were it not for the mass of **applications programs** that are available. These are programs, usually written by **software houses**, that turn your computer into accounting systems, word processors, control systems and communications terminals etc. However, these are covered in detail in the three chapters on applications.

Summary

1 Operating systems are needed to make the computer hardware easy to use. Without the operating system, even simple things like getting a character from the keyboard would be very difficult to do.
2 Operating systems are classified according to their types. Some major operating system types are batch, on-line, network and real time.
3 Batch operating systems run computers which can do different jobs one after the other. The jobs are submitted to the computer in a batch.
4 On-line operating systems give the users a reasonably quick response to what they are doing.
5 Network operating systems run networks of computers sharing resources.
6 Real time operating systems give an instant response. They are usually used in emergency situations such as missile defence systems.
7 Besides the operating systems, manufacturers usually supply utilities with their computer systems. These would include things like disc formatters and disc copying routines etc.
8 Applications programs turn the computer system into something useful for particular applications such as an accounting system or word processor etc.

Revision questions

1 Why are operating systems needed?
2 What is a **batch operating system**?
3 Why are real time operating systems sometimes needed?
4 What are **utilities**?
5 Name three different utilities that you may get when buying a computer system.
6 Would an on-line or batch operating system be best for running a computer that is used for travel enquiries such as airline bookings?
7 Why are applications programs often needed in business?
8 Make a list of five typical applications programs.
9 Would these be multi-access, batch processing or real time?
  (a) Warehouses linked to head office.
  (b) A large firm using tags on clothing.
  (c) A water board's flood-warning system.

15 Information retrieval systems

Aims of the chapter

After reading through this chapter you should be able to understand:

1 Manual and computer-based information systems and databases.
2 TV-based information systems.
3 Telephone-based information systems.
4 The terms acoustic coupler and modem.
5 Computer-based information systems.

The difference between manual and computer systems

The manual way
How would you track down a criminal? Perhaps you might start by looking at some of the criminal records. For example, can you find some clues that fit the facts? Are there any fingerprints to match? Has anyone done anything similar before?

There are many different lines of investigation to pursue. The investigation may involve many phone calls and literally hundreds of people looking at information from filing cabinets all over the country. Indeed, you may even have to look abroad if the crime involved drugs or terrorism. Think how long it would take to get a piece of information in this way! Even with efficient manually operated card index systems, it could take several hours, even if people were willing and able to deal with your queries straight away.

Often it can take weeks to find clues. Hundreds, if not thousands of records will have to be searched. The people looking through must also prevent themselves getting tired and bored if they are to remain efficient.

The computer way
Type in a clue about the crime such as 'the criminal is believed to have ginger hair', and within a few minutes, thousands of records can be searched and all criminals with ginger hair printed out. Add to this the condition that the criminal was male and tall, and all records can be searched for ginger-haired tall males etc.

Computers have been used to fight crime in this way for a number of years. Criminal records on computer, together with sophisticated methods of interrogating these records, would be called a **criminal database**. This is a system where police can make use of a central system which stores a massive amount of information about criminals.

Databases do not have to be about criminals. This was only used as an example. There are databases that have been set up for libraries, banks, lawyers, travel agents, estate agents, hospitals etc. However, what they all have in common is that it is easy for users to find a lot of information about their subject. They simply ask the computer system to search the database in a way similar to that described above.

TV-based information systems

You don't have to have a complex computer system to get information from some sources. An example, is the teletext system. **Teletext** is a method where you can receive information by using a specially adapted TV receiver. The information you can get consists of several hundred pages which are transmitted along with the normal TV signal. However, when viewing a normal TV picture, this extra information can't usually be seen.

There are several main sources of information. The BBC runs **Ceefax** and the IBA runs **Oracle** and **4 Tel**. However, all systems are similar in principle.

A special keyboard (usually in the same box as the remote control for the TV) can be used to select a page of information (see Fig. 1). The pages are transmitted serially (i.e. one after the other) and you often have to wait a few seconds until the right page comes around again.

The sort of information transmitted is TV programme timetables, news, sport and weather reports, latest travel news, and bargain holidays etc. There is even a page of jokes!

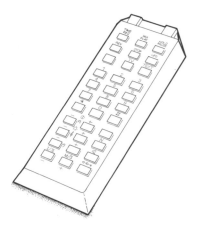

Fig. 1

Some **disadvantages** of such systems are as follows:

1 The signals are only transmitted when the TV station is on the air. That is, you can't usually get information in the middle of the night.
2 The communication is **only one way**. That is, you can't ask the computer supplying the information to do many different things.
3 The amount of information is very limited.

An **advantage** of the system is:

1 It does not cost anything to run (assuming that you already have a special teletext TV set or adaptor).

Telephone-based information systems

Many sophisticated information systems are available via the telephone. Perhaps one of the best examples in this country is British Telecom's **Prestel**.

To get information from the Prestel system you need some special hardware. This consists of a Prestel terminal and a TV set, together with an acoustic coupler or modem (see later in this chapter). However, these days more and more people are getting special software which converts their microcomputers into a Prestel terminal. Typical hardware is shown in Fig. 2.

Fig. 2

In addition to the hardware mentioned above, you will also need to be a member of Prestel. However, some schools and users, via TTNS (The Times Network for Schools) and Micronet 800, are automatically members of Prestel.

To use the system you dial a special number (which your computer can do by itself if you have the right modem), and follow instructions which appear on the screen. You will be asked to enter your customer identification number and, in addition to this, your personal passcode. This process is called **logging on**.

Once you have logged on, you will be shown a main menu. You are then free to browse through the database in many ways. One of the most direct ways is to call up a specific page number. For example, page 333 would be British Airways flight information. If you did not know the page number, you could look at the alphabetical subject index.

The amount of information stored on the Prestel database is quite large. It is well over half a million pages. A typical page is shown in Fig. 3. These pages are provided by companies who call themselves **information providers**. British Airways is one example mentioned above. Anyone who puts information on to a Prestel page is called an **IP** (information provider).

The general public cannot get some information as it is for specialist use only. An example is the travel agent's system which allows them to

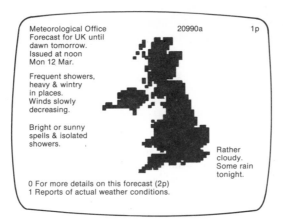

Meteorological Office
Forecast for UK until
dawn tomorrow.
Issued at noon
Mon 12 Mar.

Frequent showers,
heavy & wintry
in places.
Winds slowly
decreasing.

Bright or sunny
spells & isolated
showers.

20990a   1p

Rather
cloudy.
Some rain
tonight.

0 For more details on this forecast (2p)
1 Reports of actual weather conditions.

Fig. 3

book holidays. Only those who know the right passcodes can get at it. Other information may have to be paid for. If a charge is going to be made, then you are told how much it will be before you press the button. Sometimes, you can push a button to ask for information about the IPs product to be sent to your address, or even order goods from your home. This is known as **teleshopping**.

In addition to the charges mentioned above, you will also have to pay your subcription charge to Prestel, plus the cost of the telephone call to the Prestel computer. Although these are often charged at local rates, it is easy to use the phone for over an hour if you are looking for a lot of information or simply browsing. (The author knows of a pupil who is repaying his parents for a £250 telephone bill!) Because the charges are quite high, Prestel is mainly used by business and education. It is unusual for someone to be a member of Prestel who does not have it for business use.

One of the biggest advantages of telephone-based information systems is that it is a **two-way communication process**. Instead of just receiving information (as with the TV-based system) you can also send information. This two-way process is made use of by Prestel when using the **electronic mailbox facility**. (Electronic mail is covered in detail in one of the applications chapters later in this book.)

We have only mentioned the Prestel system but there are also others. However, they all work on very similar principles. In fact many of these other systems can be contacted from Prestel by using what is called the Gateway. This enables you to log on to and use worldwide databases from your Prestel terminal. Watch the phone bill!

The **advantages** of telephone-based information systems are:

1 It is a two-way communication process.
2 The information is available 24 hours a day, 7 days a week.
3 A massive amount of information is available.
4 Electronic mail is easily possible.

Some **disadvantages** of the system are:

1 The initial cost of the hardware.
2 The cost – there are membership, telephone and sometimes IP charges.

The terms **acoustic coupler** and **modem**

We have mentioned in the last section that acoustic couplers and modems are sometimes necessary. We now explain these terms.

The acoustic coupler
A computer can send data down the telephone line only when the data has been changed into a suitable form. One way of doing this is to make use of an **acoustic coupler** as shown in Fig. 4.

This device lets a normal telephone send signals over a telephone line by plugging the handset of the telephone into the device (as shown in Fig. 4). As the normal handset is being used, the data must be converted into sounds (that's what the telephone is designed to transmit.) The computer's binary 1s and 0s are converted into high notes or low notes. You could convert the 1s and 0s into pulses but BT would not like that. You therefore have to have a soundproof connection by pushing the handset into the rubber cups in the machine very carefully. Even so, you can sometimes get noises in the room making it difficult to transmit the information correctly. However, it **is** convenient to transmit information from anywhere in the world with a telephone. A salesman can have a small computer and an accoustic coupler in his brief case, and get up-to-date figures from head office.

The modem
This device does exactly the same thing as an acoustic coupler, but gets over the problem of noise because the telephone handset is **not** used. The **modem** (Fig. 5) plugs straight into a standard telephone socket. The modem is more reliable than the acoustic coupler, but you do need access to a plug-in socket. (For example, you can't use a modem, but you could use an acoustic coupler, with a portable computer from a phone box!)

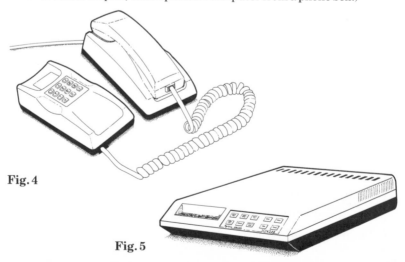

Fig. 4

Fig. 5

Computer-based information systems

We do not have to use the telephone system to get information from some computer systems (e.g. a **local computer network** in a school or business). Here, a central computer can be used as an information provider for all the local computers connected to the same network.

In the above way, companies can provide information to all employees in a more efficient way: details of meetings can be sent on an internal electronic mail facility to everyone who has to attend a meeting.

Summary

1 Computer systems are quicker and more efficient than manual information systems, due to the huge processing power of computers.
2 TV-based information systems are called teletext. Examples are Ceefax and Oracle. They do not cost very much, but are only available when TV signals are being transmitted.
3 Telephone-based information systems such as British Telecom's Prestel are more versatile than TV-based systems, owing to the two-way communication. However, they are more expensive because of extra hardware, telephone and membership charges.
4 People who provide the information on systems such as Prestel are called information providers or IPs.
5 With telephone systems such as Prestel it is possible to have electronic mail facilities and also contact other databases worldwide via the gateway.
6 Computer-based information systems are usually networks of computers connected together so that all can share the information from one or more databases connected to the network.

Revision questions

1 List three advantages that a computer database may have over a manual database.
2 What is **Ceefax**? What sort of information can be got from it?
3 Why is Prestel more versatile than teletext systems?
4 Who are the IPs and what do they do?
5 What sort of charges are made on the Prestel system?
6 Explain the term **teleshopping**.
7 Why can't teletext be used to send electronic mail?
8 Why are modems and acoustic couplers necessary?
9 Give one advantage that an acoustic coupler has over a modem, and one that a modem has over an acoustic coupler.
10 Suggest ways in which banks and building societies can use a computer based information system in a customer's home.

16 Systems analysis: is there a better way?

Aims of this chapter

After reading through this chapter you should be able to:

1 Understand what is meant by systems analysis.
2 Know the main stages of systems analysis.
3 Know what a feasibility study is.
4 Understand the information gathering stage.
K 5 Understand that a processing problem has to be solved.
6 Know why it is necessary to design input and output systems carefully.
7 Understand problems usually found with implementation of the system.
8 Understand why manuals are a vital part of the system.
9 Understand the need for a review.

What is systems analysis?

K **Systems analysis** is simply the whole process of looking at how a system in a business or a factory etc. may be reviewed, possibly for computerization. The whole process is often very complicated, and can take many months to do properly. However, without going through these stages it is likely that any computers installed will not do what everybody wants. It may even be worse than the original manual system! Many systems have been thrown out later because of this!

The main stages of systems analysis

The following sections are most easily explained by means of an example. Although large industrial companies and businesses go through similar procedures, we will look at a smaller example, which could easily happen in your school or college. We will imagine that the school librarian wants the library system computerized. We need to realize that a team of people is going to solve the problem. It is **not** one student or teacher writing a program.

We now look in detail at whether it is a good idea to computerize the library, how it is to be done, the cost of the expected system etc.

1 *Defining the problem*
The first stage is to get all the interested people together to decide exactly what is wanted. Put simply, they could make out a long list of things which the new computerized system ought to be able to do. For example:

1 It should be able to give a list of all overdue books.
2 It should be able to tell you if a book is in stock.
3 If a book has been taken, it should be able to tell you the borrower etc.

2 *Feasibility study*
The next stage is a **feasibility study** and it involves experts called **systems analysts**. These are people with great experience in computing, who can look at the problems in the above list. Given the likely amount of money you have to spend, they say if it would be possible to computerize. It may be best **not** to use computers. It is also the job of the systems analyst to point this out if necessary. The money spent employing the systems analyst would be well spent, as it is much better than installing an expensive computer system that would not work well.

At the end of the feasibility study, a **report** is written and presented to the school.

Let us assume that it **was** a good idea to computerize. (If we do not, then there would not be much more to write about in this chapter!)

The next stages will occur if it has been decided to go ahead with the project:

3 *Gathering information about the system*
The next stage is **gathering information** to find out what the **inputs** to the system are going to be. For example, what information is to be stored about each book? Title, Author, Publisher and ISBN (International Standard Book Number) might be a start.

How many books are there in the library? Does the librarian like the manual booking method being used at the moment, or is there a better way?

Hundreds of questions such as those given above would have to be asked. But how is this done in a logical way? The answer is usually for the systems analyst to carry out a lot of **interviews** with all the people that will be using the system. This must include the pupils, as they will be an important part of the system.

4 *The analysis stage*
When all the interviews have taken place, the systems analyst will then look at the problem and try to find ways of solving it. It is most important that they keep an open mind about what is being done in the system and why. You will often find that things are being done in a way which is not the best. People often do what they are told simply because it has always been done that way. Occasionally, people come up with a good idea and then everybody wonders why is was not thought of before. It is the job of the systems analyst to point out to people that better methods may exist, then convince people why they would be better. This is usually done by another series of interviews.

When the systems analyst has finally sorted out the problems generally, another report is written. This gives the possible solutions and costs, with a likely time needed to finish the project. If it is felt that the system is too expensive, then it can still be cancelled at this stage. So far no expensive hardware has been brought, and no software has yet been written, but there may be quite a bill for the systems analyst.

Again, let's suppose that we are going ahead with the project:

5 *Detailed design*
Systems flowcharts will now have to be done in great detail (remember these?). They will outline all the procedures to be done, and what files etc. will be needed. A typical part of one systems flowchart for the 'lending out books routine' might be as shown in Fig. 1.

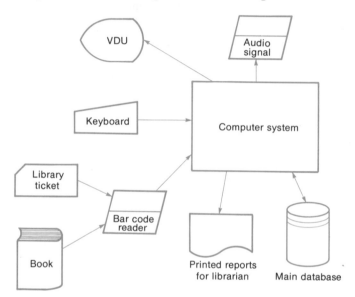

Fig. 1

These systems flowcharts are vital, as they will be used by the programmers to develop the software for the system.

Examples of some parts of the system which need careful attention are:

Data capture – getting the data in
This is a study of how data will be entered into the system (i.e. the **input**). Will any additional hardware be needed? If we are computerizing a library, then a bar code reader will probably be necessary. Or how about a laser scanner? Is this too expensive? (remember these from the chapter on input devices?).

What other forms of input will be necessary? How will the screen layout be organized when the librarian switches on the computer? Will the students be able to type information into the system? If so, what will the screens look like for them?

How will the information about Author, Publisher, Title etc. be entered into the system? Is it necessary to type in a complete name, or could searches be started from just the first few letters? Most of the problems have been covered in the detailed design section, but the **exact** way (or **format**) in which data is to be entered now needs careful attention. Get it wrong and you will find it much harder to change later.

Output
The **output** from the system also needs careful attention. What forms will be printed out if people's books are overdue? How will the information be recorded onto the file? What type of file organization will be used? (remember the work in Chapter 12?). What is the maximum size of the files going to be? What happens if the system breaks down? What manual backup is necessary if any? How will the bar codes needed in the library books be produced?

There are many details which have to be sorted out at this stage **before** any programs are actually written.

Forms for input and output will have to be designed and have the approval of the people who are going to use the system **before** any programs are written. Again interviews and lectures are very helpful and users ideas are noted.

Writing the programs
Notice how many months of work and effort have gone into the system before we have written even one line of program! How many times have you had an idea and sat down at the computer to write the program? This is **not** the way that professionals tackle problems.

The next stage of the detailed design is the **writing** of the programs. As the whole problem has already been split up into modules by the systems flowcharts, it is easy to give these modules to separate teams of programmers to be written. We only have to decide on what information has to be passed between one program module and another. People will write their separate modules and test them fully and get them working before joining them up to any other module. In this way the complicated system is more likely to work when all joined together.

Implementation of the system
After so much careful effort and design, you switch on and it works! What a pity life is not that simple. If it were, designing computer systems would be easy. The system now has to be tested fully before it is used properly.

What about typing in the thousands of titles of books that are in the library? This was obviously thought of in the design stage, but it now has to be done. Who does it? Is it the librarian? If so, who runs the library while the librarian is typing in the data? Can you get a secretary to do it? If so, who does the secretary's job?

What if the system goes wrong? (It always will sooner or later!) Should the manual system and computer system run side by side until all the bugs are ironed out? What about all the people having to do twice as much work? They thought that the computer system was going to save them work!

There will often be many problems like these. But with good systems analysis, they should be kept to a minimum. The systems analyst should have explained already that there will be time in which mistakes are to be ironed out. If people are expecting things to go wrong, then they will be more prepared for it when it happens. All problems like these, as well as things like installing the hardware, are called **implementing** the system.

Production of manuals and training
During the implementation phase (and also before it) people should be trained in how to use the system. This is especially true for the librarian, who will probably have the job of training other members of staff and students. These training sessions could take the form of lectures and practical sessions using the system.

It is also vitally important that **manuals** are produced. It is all very well to train members of staff, but what about when they leave? Who will take over?

Various types of manuals will be necessary:

User manuals
These manuals will be of a nontechnical nature, and will be intended for students and staff who will use the system. They will explain in very simple nontechnical terms how the system operates, and give specific examples of what you can do.

Manager's manuals
These will be more advanced than the user manuals mentioned above. They will be for the librarian and other key members of staff, who may have to be in charge of the system. For example, they may have to add new books that are obtained by the library, or chase up books which are overdue etc. They will be special users with more privileges than an ordinary member of staff or student. The manager's manual will therefore contain some secret information, such as 'how to assign passcodes' etc. to get into the systems files.

Technical manuals
These manuals are very complex and explain in detail exactly how the system works. They should be written in such a way that a specialist person could modify the software of the system, if this should become necessary at a later date. It must be realized that it is most likely that the people who wrote the original software may leave, and someone else might therefore have to take over the complex job of changing something. Without a good technical manual, this task would be almost impossible.

The general name for all the manuals and other similar information is **documentation**. Good documentation is as vital a part of the system as hardware and software. Without it, the system can become inefficient and eventually quite useless.

Post-implementation review, or Stop! Look! and Listen!
When the system has been installed and is working we have still not finished the job! After a month or so the systems analyst should go round

asking people if the system is OK (i.e. there should be a **post-implementation review**). Is it as good as hoped for? Does it do properly all the things that it was designed to do? Could any minor changes make life easier for the operators or users of the system? If so, can they be done easily? Although a system is never really perfect, and will always need modifications as the needs of the system change, a post-implementation review can often iron out some small but irritating problems.

Anything else?
No, but compare the above with writing programs yourself! It's a little different, isn't it? However, this is the way in which very complex projects are organized. The USA space defence system is said to have over a million lines of program! You can see that the key people in all the above are the systems analysts. Systems analysis is a vital task, as all projects of any complexity are done in this way.

Summary

1 Systems analysis is the whole task of designing a system to meet the requirements of a user.

2 A systems analyst sees that the systems analysis is done properly. They also play a major role in the implementation of the system. For larger projects there is often a team of systems analysts.

3 The problem to be solved must be well defined. This is usually the job of the systems analyst.

4 A feasibility study is carried out to see whether the computer should be used or not.

5 Gathering information about the system often needs many interviews carried out by the systems analysts. They will also observe what happens in the present system.

6 The analysis stage is a careful study to see if there are better ways of doing things or whether they need to be done at all. A report will be written which may or may not recommend computerization.

7 Detailed design then follows. This involves looking at the problems in detail, splitting them up into modules and producing systems flowcharts.

8 Careful thought is given to the way in which data is to be entered into the system (called data capture). Special forms and screen layouts may have to be designed. Extra hardware may be needed and the output section needs designing for printout of data.

9 Writing the programs and installing the hardware are the implementation phase of the problem. The programs are written from the systems flowcharts by teams of programmers. The hardware is installed and tested by engineers.

10 When the system is running, training will have to be given to the users and managers of the system. This may be done by the systems

analyst. It needs to be done well if the system is to be good and last a long time.

11 Documentation is the manuals etc. which accompany the system. Several types of manual are necessary:

user manuals for the basic users of the system;

the more technical manager's manual for people who will run the system;

technical documentation for specialist people who may have to alter the system at a later date.

12 A post-implementation review is a check later on to see that all the problems have been ironed out.

Revision questions

1 What is meant by **systems analysis** and what is the major role of the systems analyst?

2 List the main parts of the systems analysis cycle.

3 What must be done before the feasibility study can be carried out?

4 What is a feasibility study and why is it necessary?

5 Why are interviews a good method of gathering information?

6 When are detailed systems flowcharts produced?

7 From what are the programs prepared and written?

8 What is meant by the **implementation phase?**

9 What is **data capture**?

10 Why is training necessary? Who usually trains the managers of the system?

11 Why is good documentation essential and what type of documentation is necessary?

12 What is a **post-implementation review** and why is it necessary?

17 Computer people: who does what?

Aims of this chapter

After reading through this chapter you should be able to:

1 Understand why the computer industry needs many different people.

2 Understand the work carried out by the following people:

data preparation staff;   operations staff;

data control staff;   analysts;

programming staff;   technical support and research staff.

Who are computer people?

If you have used a micro only at home or at school, then it is difficult to image the role of the many computer people in industry. At home you think up your own ideas, develop your own programs, type in the code, get rid of all the **bugs** (mistakes) and use the final results yourself.

In industry, projects are far too large for one person to do all of these things. So we have teams of specialists working on different stages of projects. In a data processing application (remember this term?), you will find that there are usually many people who just type in and organize data in the system. We now look briefly at the role of some of these people.

Detailed job descriptions

Data preparation staff
In the data processing industry, there is usually a department that deals only with the entry of data into the computer system. In very large departments, there are often 50 to 100 people typing all day at VDU terminals, operating key to disc machines and verification machines (all terms with which you should be familiar!). The people who operate these machines are called **data preparation staff** because they are **preparing the data** to be entered into the computer system.

There would probably be a **data preparation supervisor** in charge of about 10 or 20 data preparation staff. In a large DP department, a **data preparation manager** would be in charge of the whole department. The data preparation manager would be responsible for making sure that the department runs smoothly, and sorting out problems with other departments in the organization.

Data control staff
The **data control staff** are in charge of collecting the data and looking after all the source and turnaround documents. (Can you remember what these are?) That is, they make sure that all the paperwork goes from and arrives at the correct places in the data processing department. The data control staff are usually split up into **data control clerks** who actually move the data round, and **data controllers** who look after and organize the data control clerks. It is the job of the data controller to make sure that only authorized jobs get done within the department!

Programming staff
The **programming staff** are the people that take the ideas from the systems analysts and convert them into a program. In the computer industry (and in the games industry!) it is very unusual for one person to write a complete program. It is usually carried out by a **team of programmers** under the supervision of a **chief programmer**.

It is the job of the programmers to produce detailed program flowcharts and any program documentation that is necessary for the system. Any bugs in the programs are sorted out by the programmers with the help of the chief programmer if necessary.

Any budding programmers should realize that many jobs are modifying existing systems, and not writing new programs from scratch.

There are two main types of programmers:

1 Applications programmers are people who program applications (e.g. useful programs like payrolls etc.) usually in a high level language.

2 Systems programmers are people who write the operating systems and utilities which improve the performance of a computer system. Systems programmers usually work using low level languages.

Operations staff

These people can be split up into the following sections:

1 Computer operators – these are people who control the hardware inside the main computer room. They do things such as make sure that the printers have paper in them, put magnetic tapes or magnetic discs into the right drives, carry out simple maintenance of the system, start up the computer in the morning (if necessary), run all the appropriate programs and keep a log of what has been going on.

Often, in large computer installations, the computer system is kept busy 24 hours a day, 7 days a week. So shift work (working at nights etc.) is often necessary for computer operators. If there is more than one operator, then it is usually split up into a **shift leader** and computer operators.

2 Shift leader – the shift leader would usually have extra duties such as preparing a timetable for the jobs to be done on the shift, and looking after the other operators. The shift leader often has meetings with other department heads, to try to improve the ways in which the computer system is being run.

3 Operations manager – this is a person who is in charge of the day-to-day running of the operations department. He or she will hire and fire staff, see that staff are trained and help to plan all the operations that are going to be done by the operations department.

Systems analysts

This department will often have several **systems analysts** under the direction of a **chief systems analyst**. These are the people who develop the projects for the customer, and decide what hardware and software is necessary. They will study the problem in great detail as described in Chapter 16.

You should realize that even after the problem has been defined, the analysts will still help the programmers with any problems, help those people who are writing the documentation and help train new staff for the customers.

All these people would be found in a large data processing department (i.e. in a place where there is a large computer system for the purpose of developing and/or running applications). Figure 1 shows how each person fits into the 'family tree' of the company under the supervision of the **data processing manager**, who is usually the boss of the whole computer organization.

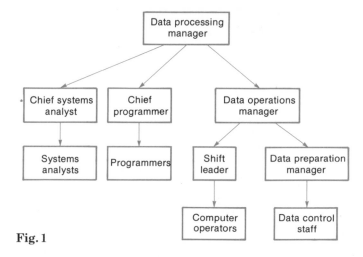

Fig. 1

So far we have only talked about large data processing departments. In small firms, one person often has to do several or all of the above jobs. However, because the firm is small this is usually not too difficult.

Technical and research staff

Technical and research staff help to develop new systems and keep the existing ones in good working order. Software as well as hardware has to be developed and maintained. These two sections are usually different departments. This is why we are considering them separately. These staff usually work for the computer manufacturers and not the data processing staff with the computer users.

Maintenance engineers – if a hardware fault develops in a system, then it is the job of the maintenance engineer to visit the computer site and fix it. Usually it is a case of changing a faulty electronic board, and the actual fault is dealt with back at the computer factory. As computers are operated 24 hours a day, the maintenance engineer often has to work shifts.

Installation (or **commissioning**) **engineers** – these engineers install the hardware for a new computer site. This can often take weeks or even months. It is often called **commissioning** the system. These engineers would make sure that the system is working properly before leaving.

Development engineers – development engineers and scientists are usually based at head office of a large computer manufacturer. They would be developing new ideas like getting more components on to a single chip or making the computers go faster.

Software development engineers – these are the people that develop the software for the new computer system. They take the latest hardware and develop powerful ways of using it efficiently, so that the system is easy to use by the customer. A good example is the use of icons and pull-down menus that enable computers to be used more easily.

Research engineers and **scientists** – finally, these are the people who are thinking up new techniques that might be useful for computers in 10 or 20 years time. Their work is highly theoretical but it is obviously the basis of the new computers of the future.

Summary

1 In large computer organizations many different jobs are performed by hundreds of different people. These people have well-defined job descriptions. However, in a small organization one or two people may have to cover many of these roles.
2 Data preparation staff look after the input of data to a computer system. They will consist of keyboard operators and data preparation supervisors under control of a data preparation manager.
3 The data control staff control the movement of data and make sure that the right data is in the right place at the right time. There are usually several data control clerks under the supervision of a data controller.
4 Computer programmers are the people who write the computer programs from the systems flowcharts given to them by the systems analysts. They are split up into applications programmers who work with high level languages, and systems programmers who work with low level languages. Each system would be under the direction of a chief programmer.
5 The operations staff consist of computer operators under the control of a shift leader, who supervises the operators during a shift. These people make sure that the day-to-day running of the computer system goes smoothly. In large departments with many computer operators there would also be an operations manager.
6 The systems analysis department would consist of systems analysts under the control of a chief systems analyst. The task of this department is described in detail in Chapter 16.
7 Technical support staff consist of maintenance engineers who repair broken down systems, commissioning engineers who install new hardware, and hardware and software development engineers who develop new hardware and software.
8 Research staff consist of research engineers and scientists who think up new ideas for the future computer systems yet to be developed.

Revision questions

1 Briefly describe the jobs of two different people in the data preparation department.
2 What does a data control clerk do?
3 What is an applications programmer?
4 What type of language would a systems programmer use?
5 The programmers usually receive their instructions from a chief programmer. However, who usually explains to the chief programmer what is to be done?
6 Why is it necessary to have many people working on a single program?
7 Who usually produces program flowcharts and who usually produces systems flowcharts?

8 Give a brief description of the operations department in a large data processing installation.

9 Why do computer operators have to work shifts? Give three different jobs that would be done by a computer operator.

10 Very briefly, list some of the things that a systems analyst would have to do. (Hint, see Chapter 16 if you have forgotten.)

11 Who would install the hardware of a large new computer system?

12 A computer system has been installed and working for a few months, but then breaks down. Who could repair it?

13 Who thinks up new ideas that might be useful for computer systems in the far future?

14 Who would design a new operating system for a brand new computer?

15 Suggest two jobs in computing that someone might be able to get with two GCSE grade Cs.

18 Process control systems and robots

Aims of this chapter

After reading through this chapter you should be able to:

1 Understand the difference between analogue and digital.
2 Explain what is meant by process control.
3 Give some examples of process control in industry and the home.
4 Be able to give some examples of how robots are used.
5 Understand what is meant by the term feedback.

The difference between analogue and digital information

There are many examples in real life where information is continuously varying. For example, if you look at the sound patterns that make up speech, you may find that they are something like that shown in Fig. 1.

Fig. 1

These continuously varying signals are called **analogue signals**.

One of the reasons why the computer will not understand what has been said is that the computer only understands digial signals. **Digital signals** are made up of lots of binary 1s and 0s. Figure 2 shows the problem.

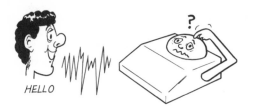

Fig. 2

If the computer is to understand the speech, an **analogue to digital (A to D) converter** is needed. The A to D converter converts the continuously varying analogue signals into binary digits that can be fed into the computer. (The computer will also need a special program if it is to understand exactly what has been said.)

Figure 3 shows how the analogue speech signal can be fed into the computer making use of an analogue to digital converter.

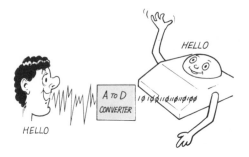

Fig. 3

Speech is only one example of an analogue signal. Other examples are: temperature, the flow of water, the distance travelled by a car, the brightness of a light bulb or the weight of a man over a year etc.

Control systems in industry and the home

It is interesting that many of these examples are measurements of some kind. This is important because most analogue to digital converters are found where a computer is used to control processes. **Process control** is the name used when computers control industrial and other processes with little human intervention. Process control might involve controlling the temperature or the flow of a liquid in a pipe etc.

Figure 4 shows a process control application where the computer is used to monitor the temperature of a power station. Often computers are used in this way to do jobs that would be very boring or dangerous for people. Imagine looking at a thermometer all day. You would probably fall asleep!

Figure 4 shows the normal operation of the power station. Water is being pumped around the heat unit so that it produces the steam to drive the generator. The computer monitors the temperature of the heat unit and adjusts a valve in case more or less cooling is necessary.

Figure 5 shows that a leak has occurred in one of the pipes. This means that not enough water is being pumped around the circuit and the temperature rises. When the temperature gets too hot the computer can sound the alarms and turn off the heat unit until engineers can repair the damaged pipe.

Notice that analogue to digital converters are needed so that the analogue signals such as temperature and flow of water could be fed into the computer as digital signals.

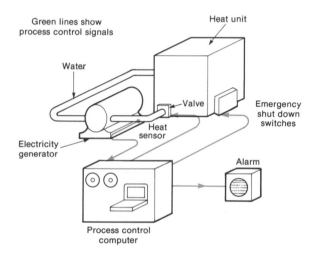

Fig. 4

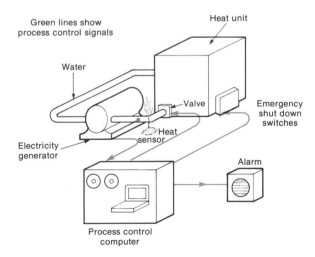

Fig. 5

Domestic process control

We do not have to go into the world of power stations to find computers controlling processes. If you have a modern electronic washing machine then a microprocessor (computer on a chip) is probably being used.

Inside the chip there will be instructions that cause the machine to go through a series of actions depending on which switches have been pressed by the person operating the machine. For example, when washing very dirty white clothes, it may be necessary to use the following programme:

Programme for dirty whites

1 Heat up water in the tub until very hot temperature is reached.
2 Agitate the tub for 10 minutes.
3 Empty tub of dirty water.
4 Fill up tub with warm water.
5 Agitate tub for 5 minutes.

6 Empty tub of water.
7 Do three rinses.
8 Slow spin for 1 minute.
9 Fast spin for 3 minutes.
10 Switch off.

The microprocessor inside the machine will be testing the temperature of the water, opening and closing the valves and spinning the tub etc. It does this by sending out digital signals to special electronic boxes which control the heater, valves and motors. The whole control process can be seen in Fig. 6.

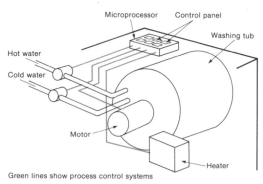

Fig. 6

Microprocessors are now finding their way into record players (to play selections of tracks from an LP), cars (to determine when a service is necessary), central heating systems (to give more economic control of heat) and many other applications.

Robotics

We are still a long way off from the days when a robot can imitate a human being in every way. However, after studying computing you should realize that this is **not** the aim of robots that are produced today.

You will find today's robots look nothing like people, although many of them are capable of doing jobs that used to be carried out by people.

Robots tend to be built to specialize in doing one particular thing. For example they may insert windscreens into cars, or move equipment around from one part of the factory to another. These are called **industrial robots** and are shown in Figs. 7 and 8.

Other types of robots are designed to go into places that would be very hostile to humans (e.g. to build a space station, or land on the surface of Mars). These robots can be controlled from computers, or act as an extension to the arms of people. An example of this last type of robot could be one that recovers lost items from the bottom of the ocean. These types of robot are controlled from a special unit on board ship.

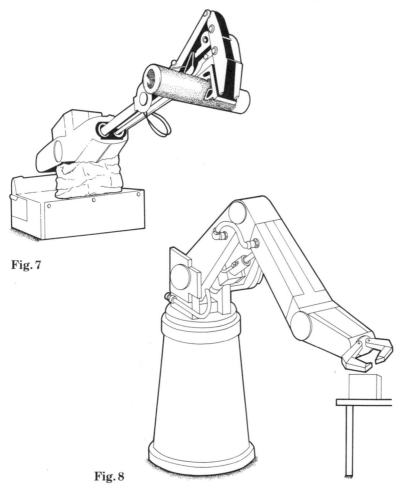

Fig. 7

Fig. 8

Domestic robots

Several companies have made toy robots which are designed to mimic human behaviour in a limited form. For example, the Omnibot and Hero robots are shown in Figs. 9 and 10. Even robot 'dogs' have been made for 'pets', house trained or otherwise!

Fig. 9 Omnibot   **Fig. 10** Hero

Both robots have an onboard computer that can be programmed to enable the robot to carry out a specific set of manoeuvres. For example, you could program the robots to go over to the drinks cabinet and fetch you a drop of your favourite wonder juice.

Let's suppose that you have programmed your robot to get the drinks by moving so many steps forward, then left, right etc. As long as the furniture in the room was not moved, the robot would not bump into anything. However, suppose that a chair was put in the way, would your program cope? The robot would probably try to walk through the chair!

There are ways of sensing when the robot bumps into an object. Signals from bumpers could be fed back into the computer, then some action is taken. This idea is an important part of robotics and is called **feedback**.

Feedback is simply the signals (got from various sensing units) that enable the robot to know where it is by being able to sense its surroundings. These signals are then **fed back** to the computer so that the robot can take the necessary action. It is easy to fit a robot with a TV camera so that it can 'see', but very difficult to get it to understand what it is seeing.

An example of feedback is shown in Fig. 11. Here you can see that a light signal from the beer mug reaches the eye which is then relayed to the brain. A signal from the brain is then used to control the arm so that the mug moves towards the mouth. This process is then repeated until the mug reaches the mouth. The whole process is usually successful as long as not much of the beer has already been drunk! This may make you wonder at the complexity of feedback systems in the human body.

SIGNAL
FROM EYE
TO BRAIN

BRAIN

LIGHT FROM
BEER MUG
REACHES EYE

SIGNAL
FROM BRAIN
TO MOVE
ARM

ARM MOVES MUG
TOWARDS MOUTH

Fig. 11

You should be able to identify feedback in many other process control applications such as controlling the speed of an electric motor, controlling the level of liquid in a tank or keeping the volume of the record player at a constant level. All of the processes can be controlled using a computer if the correct feedback signals are used.

Summary

1 Analogue signals are continuously varying. Examples include temperature, speech or distance travelled by a car.

2 Digital signals are made up from binary 1s and 0s. Digital signals do **not** continuously vary. An example of a device that would produce a digital signal is the keyboard on a calculator.

3 Special machines called analogue to digital converters are needed if analogue signals are to be fed into a computer. Computers only understand digital signals.

4 Process control is the controlling of processes like keeping temperatures constant or controlling the thickness of pastry coming out of rollers etc.

5 Domestic process control includes controlling devices such as washing machines, videos and microwave ovens.

6 Microprocessor chips are very well suited to process control jobs.

7 Robots are split up into industrial and domestic types.

8 Industrial robots are designed to do a limited set of special tasks.

9 Domestic robots are designed to mimic humans.

10 Robots can't sense what is going on around them without feedback.

Revision questions

1 Which of the following information is analogue?
(a) Speech. (b) The number of heart beats (c) The weight of a man.

2 Would a microprocessor be useful in the following and why?
(a) A microwave oven. (b) A teletext TV set. (c) A Robot.

3 (a) What is the name given to the system where computers control processes with a minimum of human help?
(b) Why are computers used to control industrial processes that used to be controlled by people?

4 There are many different types of robots today which can perform different jobs. These include shearing sheep, painting cars, or driving remotely controlled vehicles. Why is it not possible to get one robot to do everything?

5 (a) Your sponge cake begins to scorch.
(b) There is black ice on the road in front of your car.
Suggest what detector and feedback could control each example.

19 Applications of computers: look how clever we are!

Aims of this chapter

After reading through this chapter you should be able to understand some basic principles of the following applications:

1 Stock control.
2 Airline bookings.
3 Payroll.
4 Word processing.
5 Electronic mail.

Stock control

Stock control in a shop involves checking all the goods and making sure that new stock is ordered when necessary. In the past, this has meant people counting up 'tins of beans' etc. on the shelf and writing out and sending off an order to the supplier if more were needed.

Bar codes and data recorders
Bar codes (remember these?) have been a great help with stock control applications. In a simple system, a data recorder with a bar code reader attached to it can be used by staff to scan the bar code on a product. This saves the bother of having to write down a lot of information about the product. All the shopkeeper then has to do is to type the quantity of each item into the key pad on the data recorder.

The data recorder can then be used to send information to the computer system so that more goods may be ordered if necessary.

POS terminals
Much more sophisticated stock-taking systems can be found in modern supermarkets. A **POS (point of sale) terminal** is at each checkout. These POS terminals are connected to the supermarket's computer system. Each POS terminal is equipped with a bar code reader or, more recently, a **laser scanner** can be used to read the bar codes automatically.

When goods with bar codes pass through the POS terminal the laser scanner reads the bar code and passes information onto the computer system automatically. This information is used to tell the computer system that this item of stock has just been sold. This eliminates the need for someone to go around checking the shelves as described above.

At the same time that the bar code is read, information in the POS terminal is used to generate an itemized receipt. This simply means that each item of goods that you buy is automatically written out on the customer's till receipt.

There are some items that do not yet have bar codes on them. These are dealt with by the checkout person typing in either the price or a special code into the POS terminal keyboard.

Some systems are now so sophisticated that, not only can the computer generate all the order forms to send to the suppliers, but they can also contact the supplier's computer system and order the goods automatically. The idea is shown in Fig. 1 (overleaf).

In Fig. 1 you can see the person at the POS terminal with the goods, the link between the POS terminal and the store's computer system, the link between the store's computer and the supplier's computer, and finally, action being taken in the supplier's company to despatch the goods to the supermarket.

There are also some factories that have robots making and collecting the goods ready for despatch by lorry!

Another addition to the POS terminal is the ability to place a credit card or other special store card into the machine, which then debits the customer's bank account, or sends them a monthly bill. In this way, cash will be less necessary when you visit stores such as large supermarkets.

You would be right in thinking that some of the above is very sophisticated. However, it is important for companies, shops etc. to be able to keep the minimum stock levels that are possible to satisfy customer demand. If you keep too much stock, then you will need extra space to store it and thus the range of goods you can offer will be more limited. Keep too little stock, and customers will go elsewhere because they can't get the goods at your store. So you should be able to see why computers can be useful, especially in very large supermarkets and department stores.

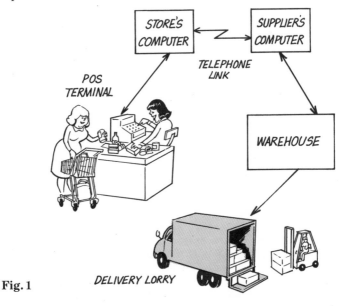

Fig. 1

Airline bookings

Have you ever thought how you can book an airline ticket for a seat on a plane from anywhere in the world? Amazing isn't it! Without complex computer systems this would not be possible.

Good communication between computers is the real key to why the airlines have been so successful. Consider the following situation:

British Airways flight BA 165 from London Heathrow to New York on 28 March has just two seats left. You are in a Leeds travel agent wanting to book your seat on this flight! If you make a quick decision, it is possible for the Leeds travel agent to confirm the booking, and the British Airways computer would be instantly updated to show that there is only one seat left. So when a couple in Bristol try to book, even though it may only be a minute later, they will be told that there is only one seat left.

The travel agent's computers are linked via networks to the airline's computer systems. In this way, a more efficient booking system is possible, and the cost of a ticket is kept as low as possible.

Not only the booking of the seats has been computerized, but also the flight scheduling (i.e. arranging the times of flights etc.), seeing to all the aircraft servicing such as food, fuel, spare parts and safety checks, arranging the crew schedules, working out wages, controlling the flight arrival and departure display boards etc. etc. All these processes and more have been computerized with the idea of increased efficiency. Without computers, the airlines would not run at all. This area is so large that many projects would be needed to cover it all.

Payroll systems

This use of computers is dear to most peoples heart! That is, how much money are you going to get at the end of the week? There are many commercial packages that are available for different computers. However, they all have things in common.

This is an application of files. Therefore, Chapter 12 should be well understood before reading further.

Data capture
Data such as the number of hours worked each week must be fed into the computer system. There are various ways of doing this but two methods are common:

1 Filling in a time sheet.
2 Using clock cards.

When time sheets are used, the data from them must be typed into the computer system at a later date by the data entry staff. However, if a clock card is used, then this produces data that is already in machine readable form.

There must also be a lot of data that is needed such as rates of pay, overtime rates, tax codes etc. However, as these do not change very often, they are not entered each week but stored on a backing store such as disc until needed by the payroll program.

The main processing
This is shown in Fig. 2 (overleaf).

After the data from the time sheets or clock cards has been read in, verified and validated, (remember these terms?) the main part of the processing begins. This involves getting information such as tax codes, hourly rates, tax to date etc. from the files as shown in Fig. 2. During the processing part of the program, master files will be updated ready for the next week's computer run.

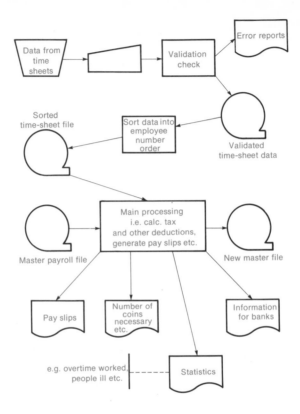

Fig. 2

The output

After the calculations have been worked out, the computer must output information to produce the wage slips. These are slips of paper given to each employee so that they know their wages and any deductions that have been made.

In addition to the above, some employees have their money paid straight into their bank account. The computer must set up the necessary transactions. If employees are paid cash, then the computer can produce what total amount of money will be needed by the pay clerk (even down to how many coins of each type will be necessary).

There are also many statistics that can be got from a typical pay run. That is,

How much overtime was worked?
How many employees worked overtime?
What was the average overtime/employee?
What is the average pay?
What was the highest pay?
How many people were off sick? etc.

Based on the above figures, management can make decisions about how efficient the workforce is in terms of value for money, if enough work is getting done on time etc.

You should be able to see from the above that working out the wages would be time consuming, very tedious and boring if done by hand, as it often is. However, when done by computer, it is accurate, does not take very much time, and masses of useful statistics can be obtained very easily.

Word processing and the electronic office

Word processing has literally changed the way that many offices are organized. Much more typing can now be done by less people than was possible in the days when typewriters ruled the office world. But first, let us look at what a word processor is.

Basic ideas
When using a typewriter you type the text on to a piece of paper. Make a mistake, and you will have to start again, or use a white correction fluid. If you need to insert a sentence into the middle of an already completed paragraph, then you are in real trouble! Instead of typing text directly on to paper, **word processors** allow you to type text on to a computer screen. Because the screen does not make permanent copy, and because it is under the control of a computer, any mistakes can easily be changed.

Word processors have two quite different modes of operation. These are as follows.

Editing mode
In this mode, text typed into the computer appears on the screen. You can alter it, add to it, delete text, move great chunks of text about and generally change the document until it's in exactly the form that you require. This mode alone does far more than even the most complex electronic typewriters.

Command mode
This is a powerful mode that enables you to give instructions to the word processor. For example, suppose that you have typed in a letter for the school magazine. It may be that each line in the letter is too long to fit into the space in a narrow column on the back page. If you were working directly on to paper, you would have to type it in again using a different line length. However, if you give a simple command to the word processor, then at the push of a button, the letter is automatically set out with the shorter line length. Have you got it right? Then instruct the word processor to print it out.

Spelling checkers
There are many other advanced facilities and one of these is usually a **spelling checker**. Even the most humble of word processor systems now

usually boasts one or two different spelling checkers. The ideas are quite simple.

The computer has a dictionary of words, usually held on disc or in ROM, (remember what ROM is?). The computer then works through the text to be checked, and, if it finds a word that is **not** in the dictionary, will bring this to the attention of the user. You can usually add it to the dictionary if it is correctly spelt, or alter it if you have made a mistake.

As the computer is comparing the words letter by letter, you can build up dictionaries of foreign languages or special technical terms very easily.

Electronic mail

If you have typed your text into a computer system, why bother to get it printed out on a printer, put into an envelope and sent through the normal post? This is often a slow process, taking from one day to a week depending on the time of year and where it is going.

Why not get your computer to send the letter electronically? The ideas behind **electronic mail** are quite simple. However, the people that you are sending the letter to must also have a computer!

Let us use the Prestel electronic mail system as an example. If you are a member of Prestel, then you can also apply for what is called an **electronic mail box**. This is really a place on a large computer where your letters can be stored.

When someone wants to send you a letter, they need to know your mail box number. After they have written the letter, they instruct the computer to send it to you by quoting your mail box number.

At some time later, you can find out from the computer if you have any mail that has not been read. It will tell you if you have. You can then read the letter from your friend and print out a copy if you wish.

Summary

We have looked at a whole range of applications, some of these are:
1 Stock control where computers can do a lot of tedious and boring work. This means that companies can keep lower stocks and also get up-to-date statistics. Special hardware such as bar code readers and POS terminals help stock control in large shops and factories.
2 Airlines use computers in many ways. Booking tickets is one where computers are linked together in a huge information service for travel agents world wide. The computers must access the information very quickly and confirm bookings from anywhere in the world. Computers are used as well by airlines for crew and maintenance scheduling, stock control, flight timetables and many others.
3 Payroll applications in many companies are used to work out wages, give management useful statistics, such as how much overtime and how many people are ill etc. Special machines for data capture such as clock cards are often used. The computer can also work out exact coins for paying weekly staff.

4 Word processing is a very sophisticated and efficient way of processing text. The computer can allow the user to edit text easily, change the form of the layout, check spelling and many other sophisticated things.

5 Electronic mail is a system where one computer can send messages to another, usually via the telephone system. One system uses a third, larger computer to store the letters in what are called electronic mail boxes and probably big firms will use ordinary letters less and less.

Revision questions and projects (denoted by*)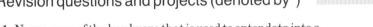

1 Name some of the hardware that is used to enter data into a computer system used for stock control in a supermarket.

2 List three advantages of computerized stock control when compared with manual methods. Also list three disadvantages.

*3 Find out as much information as you can about a computerized stock control system that is **not** in a supermarket.
e.g. In an engineering factory or in a library etc. etc.

4 Why are computers important to airlines?

*5 Find out how it is possible for travel agents to book some airline tickets via Prestel, but it is not possible for you, even if you are a member of Prestel.

6 List two different ways of getting data into a payroll program.

7 What sort of validation (see page 58) do you think would be necessary when using a payroll program?

8 Give one advantage of electronic mail over the conventional postage system.

9 Why would some post office workers object to electronic mail?

10 List two things that could **not** be sent by electronic mail.

11 A count of the items on the shelves disagrees with the computer stock record. Why might this be?

20 More applications of computers: look how clever we are again!

Aims of this chapter

After reading through this chapter you should be able to understand some basic principles of the following applications:

1 Scientific and engineering.
2 Medical.
3 Civil engineering.
4 Data logging.
5 CAD (computer-aided design).
6 Simulations.

Scientific and engineering

Do you want to design a car, build a bridge, or invent a new computer? Do you want to simulate an aircraft crashing, grow better flowers in a greenhouse, or look after 20 patients in an intensive care ward? All these and many more can be found in scientific and engineering applications of computers.

You can imagine from the above that the computer systems mentioned would need a lot of expensive hardware connected to them to be able to carry out these very specialized jobs.

While whole books can be written on each application, in this chapter we will outline just a few basic principles.

Medical applications

Computers are often found in hospitals performing a variety of tasks. Besides the normal administration, payroll and stock control applications covered in chapter 19, we will look at two other types of applications used in hospitals.

Expert systems
Have you ever wondered how a doctor arrives at a diagnosis? (That is, how they can tell what is wrong with you?) First, there is a lot of data to be gathered. For example, have you got a pain? If so, where? Are you running a temperature? Have you been sick? etc. etc.

As well as the answers to the above questions, the doctor may also take your pulse, blood pressure or other more specialized measurements such as ECG (measurement of heart activity).

When all the data has been gathered, the doctors will use their considerable experience to try and find out what is wrong. Often it will be obvious if the symptoms are common. Occasionally it will not be easy and the doctor may consult a colleague, or ask for more tests to be done. They may even need to send you to a consultant or a specialist.

If you think carefully about the above, you will see that it is simply a question and answer type of process. Based on the answers that are given, the doctor will remember what illnesses fit all the facts. They will then suggest a suitable treatment.

Suppose that a team of doctors fed all they knew about many illnesses into a computer. Also suppose that the computer could ask the right sort of questions. Then based on the answers that are put into the computer, the computer could suggest likely illnesses and also ask for more data if needed. After the computer is satisfied that the facts fed in fit an illness with a very good probability, it will suggest what the illness is and a suitable treatment. This is the basis for an **expert system**.

Some people think that the above ideas are horrendous! The computer is in effect telling you what is wrong. In fact, the computer is doing exactly the same sort of thing that the doctor was doing: simply fitting facts and suggesting a possible cure.

Systems such as these have been used in many hospitals throughout the world. The computer often comes up with the appropriate illnesses faster than a team of human experts. This is not surprising as it is possible for the computer to search its data banks at a very fast rate. Compare this with humans trying to remember some rare illnesses or symptoms that only occur once in a hundred years. The computer can search the contents of hundreds of medical textbooks in seconds!

Doctors will of course never be replaced by these expert computer systems. However, they are a very reliable form of diagnosing illnesses and diseases far quicker and with more accuracy than is possible even if every expert on every illness was available in every hospital.

It is also important to realize that expert systems are not only found in hospitals. They are being used to give advice to legal experts on points of law, and are also used in the oil exploration industry to suggest where to dig for oil. Other expert systems are under development. In fact, wherever a large body of knowledge is needed to make an assessment a computer could do it better and faster.

Intensive care units

An **intensive care unit** is where patients who are extremely ill or who have been in very bad accidents can be looked after 24 hours a day. They are usually connected up to a mass of equipment that is literally keeping them alive. It is crucial that every item of equipment is monitored for faults and that all the readings from the equipment are constantly watched to see if the patient is in need of urgent attention.

Although the nurses who look after intensive care units are dedicated and have the utmost reliability in caring for the patients, it is not an easy job to monitor masses of dials and knobs for several patients all at the same time, for a shift that may last for several hours without a break. A delay of even a few seconds could be fatal.

One solution is to connect up all the electronic equipment to a computer that monitors the progress of the patients every second without losing concentration. As soon as anything goes wrong an alarm can ring and the nurse and doctors on duty can rush to the patient with all speed.

In an intensive care ward, the condition of some patients changes very little. A drastic example may be that a patient's condition does not change for 2 months! Imagine looking at all the knobs and dials, 24 hours a day, 7 days a week for 2 months! This would be very inefficient use of a nurse's or doctor's expertise and time.

The computer is often capable of looking after about 20 intensive care patients at the same time. It would only then take one or two nurses to respond to any emergency that there may be when the computer has alerted them to the dangers.

Civil engineering

Civil engineering is concerned with the design and building of bridges, roads, railways, harbours etc. and any other major projects of this kind. Again, computers are used in administration and accounting as described in Chapter 19. But the following is a typical application used in civil engineering.

PERT: we've got to get this finished on time!
Have you ever thought about building a house? Will you do all the work yourself, or will you employ some people to help you? It would be most unlikely that you are an expert bricklayer, plumber, electrician, roofer, glazier, plasterer, painter and decorator etc. What about all the building regulations, ordering all the materials and making sure that they were delivered on time? It would certainly be silly to have the wallpaper delivered before the roof has been put on!

Let's suppose that you're so good you think that you could cope with all the above problems yourself. What if you were asked to build 200 houses? What if they had to be ready within 9 months?

You can see from the above, that large projects need a lot of planning. There will often be hundreds of people to organize. How can you work out what is to be done first? If you are going to need specialist people such as plumbers and electricians then you can't give them a day's notice when you need them, you must book them weeks or months in advance. For how long will they be needed? When will they be needed? What happens if some material is not there on time? Will it affect the completion date of the project? Is the project going to go over budget? etc. These are the sorts of questions that the managers of large construction projects have to cope with daily. To help them, computer programs based on what is called PERT are used.

What on earth is PERT?
PERT stands for **Project Evaluation Review Techniques**. In principle it is an applications package (suite of computer programs) designed to help managers undertake projects of the above sort.

A lot of information regarding the project is entered into the computer. This usually involves splitting up the project into much smaller parts. For example, if you were building a house, then you lay foundations, then build the walls and put in the door and window frames, construct the roof, lay tiles on the roof, etc. There would be many hundreds of operations from installing the central heating to fitting the glass in the windows.

When typing in the information you usually have to say when in the cycle the work is to be done. For example, you can't put the roof on until the walls are built. Therefore, if the walls are not on schedule the roof will also be late. Therefore the walls would be a critical part of the job.

Other jobs might not be so critical. For example, the gardens may not have to be laid out even before the people move in.

When a subtask such as putting in window frames is specified in the project, the cost, estimated time for the task, materials and labour needed would normally be included. Each subtask would then be built up into a complex computer model covering the whole project. The computer can then estimate the total cost, bring your attention to the materials and labour that is necessary, and tell you when the people are likely to be needed.

If something goes wrong, such as material not being ready on time, the computer can be told to make a new timeable for the project so that people and materials are used efficiently. If it can't reorganize things, then the computer will point out the critical activities. These, if not completed on time, will hold up the entire project. The manager can then look at these critical tasks and make arrangements to get material from another supplier. If a task must be finished quickly, then more men might be needed than was first estimated.

Data logging

This is a sort of computerized laboratory technician! Imagine that it is one of your jobs to go round a laboratory reading data from special instruments and recording the data in a log book. Assuming that appropriate sensors can be found. Any physical thing can be measured and changed into an electrical signal that can be fed into the computer. As an example of **data logging**, consider the following.

Automatic weather station
We want to measure things such as temperature, pressure, humidity, wind speed etc. Suppose that readings are to be taken every half an hour and the results analysed on a computer system.

First you need to get the data into a form suitable to enter into the computer. We will consider the wind speed as a typical example.

For measuring wind speed, a machine called an anemometer can be constructed. This is usually something like that shown in Fig. 1.

The wind simply blows into the cups and rotates the device. A small electric generator can be attached to the rotating shaft. The output from this generator is an analogue SIGNAL (remember this from Chapter 18?). This is then fed into an analogue to digital converter so that the digital information can be fed into the computer.

The other signals for temperature etc. are treated in a similar way. The ideas can be seen in Fig. 2.

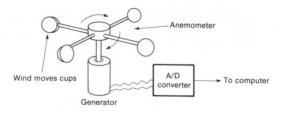

Fig. 1

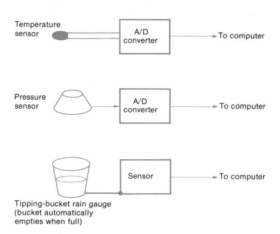

Fig. 2

Every half an hour or so, the computer would read the digital values and store them in memory. Every so often, the data would be put on to disc for future analysis. The sort of statistics that could be worked out might be the average rainfall or wind speed etc. for any day or week, the maximum and minimum temperatures reached in any period, or the number of hours sunshine per day.

The system could also give a warning of any bad conditions. For example, if the wind speed suddenly rose to force ten, the data could be read more often to warn people of the change.

Computer-aided design (CAD) and computer-aided manufacture (CAM)

Special computers with large high resolution screens and sophisticated graphics drawing facilities are used for **computer-aided design (CAD)** applications. Many things ranging from aircraft and cars to garden equipment and children's toys are often designed with the aid of a computer.

A typical example designing and manufacturing an electronic printed circuit board will now be used.

Printed circuit board design

When electronic components and chips have to be joined together it used to be done by using masses of wires. But now it is done by using copper tracks printed on a board. This is called a **printed circuit board (PCB)**. A typical simple layout is shown in Fig. 3.

When the design engineer has drawn the circuit shown in Fig. 4, this circuit can be entered into the computer system and the track layout

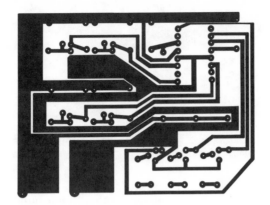

Fig. 3

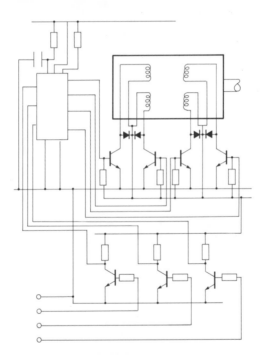

Fig. 4

shown in Fig. 3 generated by it. This takes a long time if carried out by hand, and errors can easily be made.

The next stage is to put this track on to a piece of plastic board by a photographic process. This can be done under the control of the computer system. However, we can also get the computer to help make it as well:

When a printed circuit board has been made, many tiny little holes have to be drilled into it so that the components can be fitted and soldered on. This process used to be carried out by hand or an automatic drilling machine. Suppose now that we put this automatic drilling machine under the control of a computer. All the details about where each hole has to be drilled are already there. So the computer can get the holes drilled automatically.

Not only can this be done, but the computer can also get a robot to insert the components and solder them into position. This is at the heart of **computer-aided manufacture** (**CAM**). Not only has the computer been used to design the board. It is also being used to manufacture it.

The computer knows what parts are needed for the circuit. So it can be used to produce a parts list of the pieces and order them as well.

Simulations

We have all heard of aircraft simulators. Without them the pilots of today's expensive and sophisticated aircraft could not be trained. Indeed they are so realistic that most of the pilots' initial training is done in a simulator. This is not as strange as it sounds. Think how difficult it would be to give the pilot practice in dealing with engine fires or total loss of power.

Driving simulators
The aircraft simulators mentioned above are very expensive. However, the general public may be forced to use simulators in the not too distant future. The price of a car-driving simulator is now only several tens of thousands of pounds. The use of one may be compulsory when people take their test in the future.

There are good reasons for using a simulator for part of the test. For example, you can get a child to run out in the middle of the road or get the brakes to fail on the car. You could get the computer to simulate very bad fog or to produce roads that are very icy.

People would not only be tested in the simulator, they could have a lot of practice in dealing with these difficult conditions, and a great deal of fun without doing any damage.

Summary

1 Computers are often used in scientific and engineering applications. A lot of extra expensive hardware is needed.

2 Besides general administrative work such as word processing and accounting etc., computers are found in hospitals helping with intensive care. Computer expert systems also help doctors to diagnose many diseases.

3 Many civil engineering projects use computers for design and costing of building roads and bridges etc. Besides stock control and accounting they are used for PERT (Project Evaluation and Review Techniques). This simply means that the computer can help manage the schedules, labour, costs etc. for very large and complex projects.

4 Computers are often used in a data logging role. This means that they can collect data from various instruments and work out statistics based on the results. Typical examples would be monitoring the weather or checking pollution.

5 Computer-aided design (CAD) is getting the computer to help design the plans for cars and aircraft etc. They can also help make the products by controlling the machines that do the manufacturing. In this case, it is called computer-aided manufacutre (CAM).

Revision questions and projects (denoted by*)

1 Name three different applications of computers in science and engineering.

2 What is an **expert system**? Give an example of how it can be used.

3 Why are computers useful in intensive care units in hospitals?

4 How can a computer be of any use when building a bridge? Name two entirely different computer applications which could be useful.

5 What does **PERT** mean and why is it useful?

6 What is **data logging**? Give an example where computers can be used for data logging.

7 What do **CAD** and **CAM** stand for?

8 Give one example of computers being used for CAD?

9 Give an example of where computers are used for CAM.

*10 Find out about how computers are used to help design cars.

*11 Find out about how computers are used to help manufacture cars.

*12 CAD systems are very expensive, give two reasons for and two against using them.

21 Applications of computers: we are still being very clever!

Aims of this chapter

After reading through this chapter you should be able to understand some basic principles of the following applications:

1 CAL (Computer-aided learning).
2 Education administration.
3 Home computers.
4 Computer music.
5 Computer games.

Computer-aided learning (CAL)

What a pity that this does not mean that the computer takes all the hard work out of learning! Nor does it mean that the computer will replace some of your teachers! It simply means that the computer is being used to help you learn a subject in a more imaginative way.

The very first **CAL packages** were boring and dull. Often they just asked you many different questions and you typed in the answers. Many of today's packages are more interesting and have a lot more educational value. For example, they are likely to have colour graphics and sound and are often backed up by superb documentation. (Remember what this is?) Some packages even have computer-generated speech.

Human teachers can run out of patience, but the computer never will. If you find the questions too hard, it can make them easier. It can also give help when needed and check your answers right away. Each pupil gets the help they need, when they need it. In industry the computer is used to teach safe habits, how to fill in forms, and how to improve your manner on the telephone.

The range of subjects covered is enormous. Anything from French and German to geography and computer studies. Often, because the computer is in control, learning can be made quite a lot of fun and is often regarded by younger people as a game. This is especially true of some of the historical simulations where the computer asks the user to make some of the decisions in some famous battle. Even the adults can't resist being the general for a time!

Battle strategies can be learnt and often you can gain a good idea of why some of the historical decisions were made. Also, you can often realize that very bad decisions were made. This is usually more interesting for children than simply reading a book or looking at a video because the computer is **interactive**. That is, it enables the user to make some of the decisions that affects what is going to happen.

With the invention of the optical disc, video quality images can be presented on the computer screen under the control of the computer. The laser disc can therefore link video and computer technology to produce truly amazing computer-aided learning packages.

Educational administration

If the teachers think that computer studies are important then it is only right that all these wonderful machines ought to be helping them with running the school. This is indeed the case in many schools.

A few years ago **educational administration** was only carried out by the few members of staff who were brave enough to program the computers themselves. Although this still goes on to some extent, many professionally written packages are now available that have been written with school administration in mind. These packages range from sorting names into alphabetical order to quite large and sophisticated databases storing many files of information about pupils. This ranges from names and addresses, telephone numbers etc. to examination results. There are also programs to help with the horrendous tasks of producing the timetable. Although some heads believe that it is quicker to do it by hand!

One big advantage of having information such as 'who is teaching who and in what form' etc. is when it comes to planning trips. For example, suppose that the geography department is planning a field trip for the fourth-form geographers and wants to get the parents' permission.

On a manual system this would mean collecting together all the lists from the teachers who teach geography to the fourth form. Next you would have to go to the office and find out all the names and addresses of the parents to whom the letters are to be sent. (Never rely on the pupils, the letters might never get home!) Finally, the secretary would have to type out and address all the envelopes and send off each one with the letter inside.

Using the computer system, it would be possible to tell it to search the files for all fourth-form geographers, find the names and addresses of all these pupils and get them printed out on address labels on the printer.

The above are only two examples of the hundreds of ways in which computers can be used to help teachers run the schools. More applications are being thought up every day.

Home computers

Several million people have got **home computers**. In this country we have more computers per 100 people than anywhere else in the world. How many people do you think make use of them regularly? Would the number you thought of go down if you did not count the times that they are used by children to play games? I think it would!

There are many serious **applications programs** that are available for home computers. These range from word processing and home accounts, which can be used for club records, through computer-aided learning (see the beginning of this chapter) to computer art packages that make use of a mouse. One of the disadvantages about using home computers is that they have to be bought out of your own money. Even though the computers are the least expensive there are, several hundred pounds is still a large amount of money for many people to find. This is especially so when the extra programs they might need could also cost several hundred pounds. Add to this the fact that many people don't understand how to use them. It is little wonder why so many households end up with the computer just used for playing games. Also, many are left in their boxes because the children have got fed up with them.

However, there are also many people who do take time to learn the system and are able to get the computer to do many clever and amazing things. Such people have often learnt about computers at home, and then got enthusiastic about them and gone on to work in the computer industry.

The other type of person who uses home computers a lot are people like authors who write their books on word processors, business men who use them to keep in touch with systems such as Prestel and programmers etc. who work from home. In fact working from home is now becoming quite popular, especially with working mothers. They can stay at home and look after the children while at the same time they can do their work via the home computer system, at times which suit them.

Computer music

At the lowest level, **computer music** could simply mean writing a BASIC program which makes use of the sound commands that may be present on your computer system. However, unless you are very good at programming it is unlikely that this would be very sophisticated or easy to use.

There are several applications packages on the market which turn your computer keyboard into a musical instrument. These programs usually have very good graphics and enable you to change the sounds that the computer makes very easily. Some programs will enable you to play several tracks at once and record another track while you are playing back and listening to another. This is indeed quite clever. However, the severe limitation on all of these types of programs is the ability of your computer to produce a good sound, and most of all, the unnatural way of using the computer keyboard.

The most sophisticated musical packages are the ones where your computer controls a proper music synthesizer. This would be a full-sized musical keyboard that plugs into your computer via an interface called **midi** (**m**usical **i**nstrument **d**igital **i**nterface). This is a standard interface which means that many different keyboards and other machines such as drum synthesizers could all be connected to your computer.

The sounds that some of these synthesizers make are unbelievably good. They are exactly the same as the sort you see pop groups using live. Indeed some pop groups are now using microcomputers to play some of the music that they use in their act.

You can usually use the computer to play music via the keyboard or to edit out any of the mistakes that you may have made when the music was originally recorded using the computer.

This option is now becoming so popular that some microcomputers are being supplied with a **midi** interface as standard.

Computer games

Yes, the author must admit, on occasions he has played the odd computer game, or two or three!

Computer games are a great source of fun and enjoyment. They can waste a lot of time if you get addicted. But if used sensibly can also teach you a lot of keyboard skills. There can't be many children in the country that don't now what a RETURN, NEW LINE or ENTRY KEY is on a computer keyboard.

Several years ago computer games were limited to the space invaders zap-em-or-die type games. Although amusing for a time, people soon become bored and wanted more complicated games.

To get very advanced games with excellent graphics and sound etc. you had to wait until more sophisticated and powerful home microcomputers were available. Sixteen-bit micros such as the Commodore Amiga and the Atari 1040ST saw a fantastic leap in the realism and complexity of computer games. The next generation (e.g. the Archimedes) will be even better.

The next stage will come when the laser disc can be easily interfaced to the computer and you get interactive video. (This is very expensive at the moment; the BBC Domesday Project is a good examples of the start of this technology.) You can then imagine that the computer can control the television-type images for realistic games such as flight simulators etc.

Summary

1 Computer-aided learning (CAL) uses computers to make interactive learning more exciting than is possible with books or film, with immediate help and feedback.
2 Computers can be used in schools for storing information about pupils and helping teachers with the timetable. Lists can be searched, which is very useful for printing out lists for staff (e.g. all pupils who were absent on Thursday or all who are studying computing in the fifth form).
3 Home computers are used for many serious applications. They often help people to work from home or get information from larger computer systems such as Prestel etc. If not used seriously, people often get fed up with them.
4 Home computers are good for generating musical sounds. With the right software and MIDI interface, they can be used to control sophisticated musical instruments.
5 The latest computer games are now very sophisticated. With the powerful microcomputers coming into the home, and powerful laser discs that can be computer controlled, the future looks exciting.

Revision questions

1 What is meant by the term CAL?
2 What advantages do good CAL packages have over standard text books and films?
3 Name four quite different uses of computers in administration at school.
4 A school stores much information about its pupils on computer. Suggest how combinations of information could be of use to three different members of staff or parents.
5 Name some of the types of people who make much use of home computers. In each case, give example of the main use of the computer system.
6 Why can a home computer cost much more than was originally intended? Give some example of the jobs that some people may wish to do, and the extra equipment that would be necessary to add to the computer system to do it.
7 Why have more powerful microcomputers been necessary to make computer games more exciting?

22 Case studies

Aims of the chapter

After reading through this chapter you should be able to:

1 Understand what is meant by a case study.
2 Go through and understand a simple case study.

What is a case study

A **case study** is simply a detailed look at how computers are used in a particular application. Case studies are usually left to late in your course, as it is a way of revising and extending what you have learnt throughout the course. It will join together many aspects of computers and show you how they are used in the real world.

Some examination groups require that you undertake one or more case studies throughout your course. In fact there is sometimes a separate exam paper on a case study. This chapter will present and lead you through a typical exam type case study. **Questions will be asked throughout the chapter and therefore there will not be any questions at the end**.

It is far better, if possible, to visit a computer installation that you have done a case study on. However, this takes a lot of time and effort and can't always be arranged.

Example case study

The Drive-You-Mad car company
The Drive-You-Mad car hire company has a nationwide network of car hire facilities in most large towns throughout Britain. The company has tried to introduce a policy which allows drivers to collect a car at any one of these branches and return the car to any other branch. After a big advertising campaign, business is booming and the managing director is pleased with the increase in trade. There is, however, a problem. When each branch operated on an individual basis, the manager of the branch could cope easily with the allocation of cars and advance booking. But the introduction of the 'pick it up anywhere, leave it anywhere' policy has led to local branch managers being unable to know quickly how many of their cars will be at their branch at any one time. On several occasions this has led to customers not getting the car of their choice at the right time and the right place. Indeed, in some cases, the managing director has had to lend out his Rolls-Royce to prevent customers from being disappointed.

A better organization of the data on a national basis is therefore required, and the 'We Get It Done' computer consultants were called in to computerize the system.

After extensive systems analysis, it was decided to have a nationwide system of computers, linked up to a larger computer at central head office in Birmingham. Each region of the country would have a regional head office, with all the local branch office computers connected to it. The idea is shown in Fig. 1.

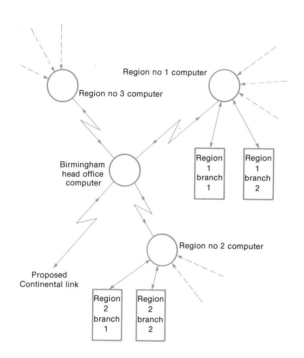

Fig. 1

Revision questions

1 State one reason which led to the firm of 'We Get It Done' computer consultants being brought in.
2 The 'We Get It Done' computer consultants carried out the systems analysis. What does this mean?
3 What hardware would probably be used to enable the computers in the branch office to communicate with the computers at head office?

The requests from customers are broken down into two forms: immediate bookings where a customer demands a car at no notice and advance bookings. It is company policy to satisfy all advance bookings (i.e. cars booked more than a day ahead) with the right type of car in the right place, and try to satisfy as many immediate bookings as possible.

There are three types of cars available:

1. The economy Mini Uno, a small four-seater car.
2. The Biera, a mid-range family saloon with an 1800 c.c. engine.
3. The prestige Scorpion, a top of the range executive saloon with electric windows and seven computers (ideal for impressing the new girl or boy friend!).

Each local branch has a fleet of cars containing all the above models and the quantity of each model held by the local branch depends on the type of business in that particular area. The branch manager will try to keep a minimum number of cars to cater for local demand. It allows other cars to be allocated to different areas if necesssary.

The system must make sure that no region experiences a lack of cars and no region has so many that it can't possibly cope. The company employs a team of drivers to sort out the situation if it gets out of hand.

Revision questions

4 Would you suggest that the information about cars is held on disc or tape? What are the reasons for your decision?
5 The master file held at head office in Birmingham will be a complete record of the movements of the cars in the company. List four different items of information that you think ought to be included in the master file and why?
6 What hardware do you think will be necessary in each branch office, (i.e. an office which is connected to the regional head office)?

The 'We Get It Done' consultants decided to have a two-tier system:

1. Information at local level is to be kept on the regional computer system, and all the local files can be updated without the need to reference the master system in Birmingham.
2. The master system needs to be referred to only when a car is known to be going out of the region, or when a car has arrived from another region.

Besides acting as a regional computer for the local area, the master computer must be able to respond to emergency situations such as 'instructing the drivers that one region is running low on a particular make of car'. A printout could then be arranged that would instruct the drivers to go to a region where there are too many, and bring a car back to make up a region with too few.

A systems flowchart for the Drive-You-Mad company is shown in Fig. 2.

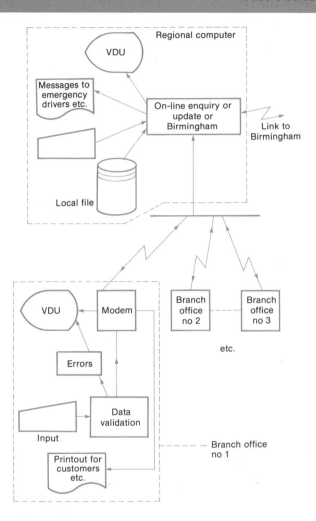

Fig. 2

Revision questions

7 At branch office level, when information is being typed into the system, there is a data validation box. What does **data validation** mean?

8 For the Drive-You-Mad car company, suggest two different pieces of data that could easily be validated.

9 A printout for the customer can be obtained from each branch office. What type of printer would you suggest is used and why?

The computer system keeps a record of the mileage that each car has done. Every 2500 miles the cars go in for a service at the garage at the regional headquarters. Also, if a car has done more than 60 000 miles, or the car is more than 3 years old, the company decides that this is not good for its image and gets rid of that particular car.

The following shows part of a record from the master file for Scorpion car:

Field	Typical contents
Key field	Scorpion 23
Registration number	E 463 YKL
Date of purchase	09/08/87
Mileage	5164
Mileage at last service	3218
Current area	Sussex

Revision questions

10 What is a key field usually used for?
11 Does the above car need a service?
12 Assuming that this Scorpion does not do very many miles, when will it be replaced by a new one?
13 What do you think could be the purpose of the number 23 in the key field?
14 Name three other vital pieces of information that would be needed if the system is to be used for car booking.

The above system has not mentioned any detail of the information necessary for the booking of cars. The booking information is stored on another file but ties up with the car master file mentioned earlier because each car has a unique identification (e.g. Scorpion number 23 in the previous section). Customers may book a car up to a maximum of 3 months ahead.

Revision questions

15 Suggest five fields that would be necessary in the car booking file.
16 What information in the booking file would you recommend to be used as a key field and why?
17 Would it be a good idea to keep booking up to 3 months in advance on disc? If so, how would you go about estimating the size of the file necessary?

The Drive-You-Mad car company is very pleased with the operation of their new computer system. They intend to extend the system so that it can help out with some other parts of their business, such as secretarial help and producing statistics.

Revision questions

18 Suggest three areas other than car booking where the computer system could be used to advantage.
19 What sort of statistics do you think would be useful to the management of the company? Give four examples.
20 What type of operating system do you think would be necessary for a customer enquiry? On-line or batch? and why?

23 Computers and society

Aims of the chapter

After reading through this chapter you should be able to understand some effects of:

1 Computers on the individual.
2 Computers on society.
3 Computers on business.

Why computers and society?

Computers affect most parts of modern life in one way or another. This is why we have to look at this important part of computer studies.

If you ask any person in the street what they think about computers, they almost always have an opinion about it. In the exam, when you are asked questions on computers and society, it is very easy to forget all that you have learnt throughout your course, and answer them in a similar way to the person in the street. However, even though you may write down a lot, without hard facts you will not get many marks. For example, just saying that you think 'computers are taking over the world' will score you nothing.

Computerization is not all bad or all good. It is up to you to think of **both** good and bad points whenever you are presenting an argument.

Computerization affects people in a different way to society and industry. We will therefore split up this chapter into different parts.

Some effects of computers on the individual

Employment

This is one area where computers have had a huge effect on the individual. Consider the following arguments:

Computers are now doing jobs in the factory that used to be done by people. Many of these people are now on the dole. If the robots and computers had **not** been introduced, then these people's jobs would have been saved.

Many people would agree with the above. However, if you think of the same argument put in a different way:

Other industries throughout the world are using robots and computers. They are producing the same goods as us, but are selling them more cheaply. People are not buying our goods because they are too expensive. We have therefore had to close down our factory and **all** of the jobs have been lost.

The above two arguments are of course very simply put, but it does show that, to remain competitive, we must keep up with the latest techniques. If we don't, then jobs are going to be lost anyway.

Computers can work for 24 hours a day, 7 days a week, 52 weeks a year. No person could hope to compete with such productivity. However, computers are not good at doing everything. What we must do is to use the computers on the jobs that they are good at (i.e. boring and repetitive tasks, or where it would be dangerous for humans to work). We can then use the humans on the jobs which they are good at (e.g. sorting out anything that goes wrong, looking after the customers or telling the computers what to do).

One thing that is obvious from the above is that the jobs people will do in the future will be very different from the jobs that they have done in the past. Also, the place of work will be different. With the introduction of more powerful microcomputers and good communications via the telephone, this has meant people can now work from home. Even today, thousands of people work from a computer terminal at home, and only go into the office when they need to meet other people. Indeed in the future, with the introduction of video telephone links, it may not be necessary to have an office at all! This would lead to a great saving in office space and time and cost of travelling.

Whether or not the above will literally come true is doubtful. This is because people actually **like** going to work and meeting other people. This is usually the place where you make friends. However, the pattern of going into work from nine in the morning until five in the afternoon will probably alter.

Leisure

Computers don't provide much leisure activity as such (with the possible exception of computer games!). What we usually mean is that because computers are doing much of the work that used to be done by people, the people now have more time to spend doing leisure activities.

One of the fastest growing industries is the leisure industry. This consists of things such as sports centres, theme parks, hotels, activity holidays and the tourist industry in general. These industries are often known as the service industries because they provide a service to the people. Some people who have lost their jobs through computerization have found employment in these service industries.

It is very true that the hundreds of thousands of jobs lost through computerization are **not** going to be replaced by those in the service industry. Also, a skilled technician in the weaving industry is probably not going to look too kindly at being offered a job of selling ice creams in a theme park!

What has probably got to be sorted out is people's attitudes towards work and leisure. People tend to identify themselves with a particular job. If you ask someone what they are, they will probably reply with 'a teacher' or 'an engineer'. Take away this identity, and you have taken away a large part of that person's pride.

Personal privacy

This is another area in which computers have had an enormous impact. There has always been information stored about people. For example, there are medical records, hire purchase agreements, bank accounts, mortgage accounts, birth certificates, school records etc.

In the past, this information has been stored on paper inside filing cabinets. To get to such information would involve going round all the offices and asking for it. (This is assuming that you were entitled to know!) It would have taken a very long time indeed to build up a file of information on a particular individual.

Today much information is stored on computer. The information is no different but the speed at which you can get it is. Assuming that you know the correct codes it would be possible, via the telephone system and another computer, to access some of the information within seconds.

It is unlikely, but it would be possible, to build up a comprehensive file about an individual very easily. This is what worries many people. What makes things slightly easier is that in the last few years there has been a trend to store more and more of this information on huge centralized data banks.

It quite rightly worries people that some information stored about them on computer may not be correct. This could be drastic if they are applying for a loan to buy a new car, for example. If they have a bad credit rating on computer (a way of telling if people are likely to pay back the money they owe), then they may be refused a loan.

The **Data Protection Act** of 1984 allows members of the public to inspect information that is stored about them on computer files. If this information is wrong, they can ask for it to be changed.

The above may sound like 'big brother is watching you' but it does also have advantages. For example, if a person was involved in a serious accident, then, even while the patient was being brought into hospital, a printout of their medical records could be produced on the hospital's computer. Any special information that the doctors may need to know (such as the patient is allergic to some forms of drugs) can be instantly available. Methods such as these could obviously save the patient's life.

Large computer data banks can also help the police in fighting crime. For example, the DVLC (Driver and Vehicle Licensing Centre) computer at Swansea has all the information about car owners in the country. Suppose that the police were following a suspected stolen car. They can radio their local office to check the computer at DVLC and within seconds the real owner of the car can be found out. The police can then stop the suspect car and ask the driver who owns it.

There are various arguments about whether it is a good thing or a bad thing to have so much information on computers. However, they can all probably be summed up by saying that it is a good thing **if the information is used properly.** Most members of society would agree with this, and efforts are being made to keep misuse of information to a minimum.

Social change

There have been huge changes in society already. There are going to be even more in the future. We have seen above the changes in employment, leisure and privacy. You should be able to produce arguments for and against each one. For example, it is all very well saying that there will be increased leisure, but what if you're unemployed and can't afford it? Similarly, it is all very well saying that more interesting jobs are being created. It is usually only the 'clever' people who end up with these jobs. What happens to all the people who enjoyed doing the tasks that the computers have taken over? Will there be a two-class society – those with jobs in computing and those without much hope of a job at all? Some people think that so much information stored on computers will lead to a 'police state' (i.e. one in which people are constantly monitored by the police).

There are many arguments for and against. Whole books have been written on each subject. The only way in which you can get a balanced view of what is going on is to talk to lots of different people. In your answers to these questions, make sure that your views are balanced too.

The effects of computers on business

A company usually has to make a profit if it is to stay in business. Anything that can sensibly cut costs is therefore usually a good idea. Computerization does cut costs. Computers take no tea breaks and do not go on strike. They enable one person to do the work of many. This is not only true in the factory, but in the office as well. We all know how word processors improve the ability of one typist to do the work of about three of four typists without these machines.

It is not only the profit motive which has forced companies to computerize. Some processes in manufacturing industries are now so complex that they could not hope to be carried out without the aid of a computer. For example, designing and building cars and aircraft, designing and building robots and other computers, controlling power stations or chemical factories and the space program to name but a few. In fact it would be true to say that most companies are now so far down the road of computerization that they can't go back. Business would literally be impossible without computers.

The above state of affairs has changed the sort of people that companies are now looking for. It is expected that people ought to be computer literate. That is, they should know the basics about computers and why they are used and needed etc. In addition to this there is a massive amount of retraining that is necessary. Computing is a rapidly changing skill and what people know today will not be enough to help them in 5 to 10 years time. Companies are therefore looking for workers whose attitude to change is positive.

Many trade unions who have resisted computerization in the past are now realizing that they have little choice. It is far better to work together with the new technology than to oppose it. Both management and workers are realizing this and the last few years has seen a drastic reduction in people who oppose computers simply because they do think that they are taking over the world.

We must use computers wisely. They are one of the most versatile things ever to be developed by us on this earth. Their potential is enormous, and only just beginning.

Summary

1 Computers affect people by affecting their: employment, leisure and privacy.

2 You should be able to produce arguments for and against in each of the categories mentioned in 1.

3 You should be able to use facts to support your arguments and **not** just rely on woolly statements such as 'I think that computers are bad because they are taking over all the jobs'. Statements such as these will get no marks in an examination.

4 You should be able to argue from the point of view of a person or the point of view of a company in business. Your arguments will be different in each case.

Revision questions

1 Why is it sometimes necessary to replace people with computers?
2 List four different jobs that have been taken over by computers?
3 Why can't all jobs be done by computers?
4 How can computers effect (a) people's leisure?
   (b) people's privacy?
5 Make a list of five different organizations that would store information

about people on computers?

6 Why are some people worried about computers storing information about them?

7 List three advantages that storing huge amounts of information about people on computers would bring.

8 Why do so many businesses use computers?

9 In simple terms, what is the Data Protection Act of 1984 meant to achieve for the individual?

10 One day, teachers may be replaced by computers. Suggest two reasons why this may be good for pupils and two reasons why it may be bad.

11 A supermarket converts its checkouts so that prices may be read by laser scanner passed over bar codes. Give two reasons for and two reasons against this from the point of view of a shop floor assistant.

24 The future: gaze into your crystal ball!

Aims of this chapter

After reading through this chapter you should be able to:

 Appreciate some of the ways in which computers might be used in the future.

The future

Stardate 1987! What do you think the world will be like in the year 2087?

To appreciate this a little more, lets go back 100 years to 1887. We need to look at some of the technology of the time. The computer had not been invented. That was to come much later. Electricity was not the common form of power. Streets were lit by gas lamps. Most people were employed in dark and dingy factories, or were farmers and labourers on the land. There were of course the upper class who lived lives of luxury with many servants to tend to their every need but these people did not form the majority of the population.

If we leap ahead by 50 years to the late 1930s, then we are between the two world wars. Electricity was becoming more common and, yes, the first electrical computer had just been invented in the form that we know it today. However, in the next few years, the computers developed were large and cumbersome machines that consumed huge amounts of power. Even the smallest of the home microcomputers today could far out-perform these huge monsters.

In the next 50 years to the present day, the computer has developed into the form that we now know it.

Fifty years is not a long time when speaking historically. It is well within a single person's lifetime. To see such great change from huge inefficient computers to small computers that have made it possible for man to land upon the moon and travel into deep space must be awe inspiring.

So what of the next 50 years? The pace of change today is such that it is reasonable to expect much more progress than in the last 50. We now have computers to help us design the next generation of computers.

The speed at which computers can calculate has increased by a huge amount. The early computers could perform only a few calculations per second. This was impressive enough in their time. But today, computers can perform millions of calculations per second. Computers can also work together so that they can share working things out between them, and thus get things done even more quickly.

The new technologies

To imagine what might happen in the next few years we have to look at what is happening in the laboratories of today.

Speech recognition

We see huge advances in **speech recognition**. Today, there are systems that can recognize the human voice over quite a large vocabulary. These laboratory systems are using powerful mainframe computers to perform the complicted analysis necessary. But in the future, owing to the increasing microminiaturization of computers, it should be possible to get the same power in the size of a briefcase.

One of the main disadvantages for humans entering data is in the use of the keyboard. When speech recognition is perfected, we will be able to talk to the computer using English, or whatever language it has been programmed to recognize. It will even be able to listen to an English voice and instantly translate it into Spanish, or any other language.

Visual recognition

Much progress has also been made in the field of **pattern recognition**. This gives computers the ability to recognize shapes. Already there is software available that can tell if a person is happy or sad, according to whether they are smiling or frowning! Again, the power of a mainframe is required for this operation at present.

The thinking machine

The next generation of machines (called the **fifth generation**) being developed will make significant advances in the field of **artificial intelligence**. These machines are to be the so-called intelligent machines. One would hope to be able to communicate with them in English, and the machine would give a good impression of thinking as humans know it today. In the past we have always had to tell computers how to solve problems by means of a program. Part of the fifth-generation thinking will involve us explaining the problem to the computer, but then getting the computer to work out a solution. If these ideas are extended, then it may be that someday computers will be thinking and solving problems that are too complex for man to think about and solve. The speed of these computers would be several thousand times as fast as the current generation of supercomputers.

Hundreds of millions of pounds are being put into the development of these new machines. Even if only part of the system is developed, the results will certainly be impressive.

Storage technology

Even faster and larger storage devices have been developed over the last few years. The advent of the **laser disc** has meant that huge amounts of data can be stored on a small disc no larger than the size of an LP record. When the problems of writing data easily to this disc have been solved, then this storage media will be even more useful than it is today. Couple this with the ability to store video quality pictures, and you have intelligent interactive video and computer programmes.

Communications

The computer has already revolutionized the way that **communications** take place. The telephone network of the world is becoming entirely digital. It will take many years to do but, when the system has gone mostly digital, computer mail will probably be the normal method of communicating with people. This is not just a fancy dream. It will literally be the cheapest method. Businesses will not go for the more expensive method of sending letters by ordinary mail, unless there are special reasons.

Computer graphics

Owing to the huge increase in speed and memory capabilities of computers, stunning **graphics** are now possible. It is now relatively easy to produce the realistic looking graphics that are used in aircraft simulators. Another 10 years will produce a realism that will be startling. Complete films are already being produced entirely by computer, and the artist of the future will really only be limited by his imagination.

What happens after silicon?

Scientists have been working with materials other than silicon in forming parts of computer systems. Perhaps the most controversial of these are the systems that actually contain living material. Experiments with protein that can reproduce itself out of genetically engineered material have found to be useful for some parts of computers! Maybe we can grow extra memory for some of our customers!

What next then?

One can see from the above that there are many exciting developments. However, it must be realized that these are just a few of the ones that we know of today. They are also being developed in isolation. Put them all together, and you have a machine that will make today's supercomputers look worse than a hand-held pocket calculator. If you know the book *The Hitchhiker's Guide to the Galaxy* you may have some idea of how small and powerful computers are likely to become. One can only wonder in amazement as some of these new developments take place and hope that in the future they will be used for the benefit and not the destruction of the human race.

Summary

1 No one can actually predict what is going to happen in the future. However, one can say that the rate of progress will be much more rapid.
2 Specific developments worthy of note are going on in the fields of:
speech recognition;
visual recognition;
fifth-generation computers;
storage technology;
computer graphics;
and communications to name but a few.

Revision questions and project (denoted by *)

1 Name three recent developments in the field of computing.
2 Name one way in which fifth-generation computers are going to be different from the current generation.
*3 Choose one recent development, such as computer graphics or voice recognition etc. and find out more about it.
4 It is the year AD 2000 and children at school have no textbooks. Suggest how this might be possible and give some reasons for and against it happening.

Answers to revision questions

Chapter 1

1 Driving a car in a busy street, copying a human being and carrying on an intelligent conversation about any subject are three things which computers can't do at the moment. (They may be able to one day!)

2 Due to the fantastic advances in the technology.

3 Keyboard, mouse, bar code reader, kimball tag, disc etc.

4 Printer, plotter, disc, VDU etc.

5 Information is what you get when meaning is applied to data.

6 Changing information from one form into another.

7 The computer only understands special codes.

8 (a) Large business or university.

(b) Large and small businesses.

(c) Small business, school and the home.

(d) Weather forecasting, the military etc.

9 A microprocessor.

10 Hardware is the equipment; software is the programs.

11 A set of instructions to tell the computer what to do.

12 To store programs and data needed at a later date.

13 The main part of the computer that controls all the operations.

14 Control unit, arithmetic unit and immediate access store.

Chapter 2

1 It can be read directly by the computer system.

2 It is slow and many errors can be made.

3 You can use it to point to icons on the screen. This saves typing.

4 Entry of data via a keyboard.

5 The processes of entering data into the computer system.

6 A machine that can read a source document directly into the computer.

7 The banking system makes use of it on the bottom of cheques.

8 A multichoice examination answer sheet.

9 It saves typing in text that is already typed out on to paper.

10 Bar code readers (wand) and laser scanners.

11 A mark sense reader.

12 It is more like a paintbrush to control than a mouse.

Chapter 3

1 Hard copy is printed out; soft copy is on the VDU screen.

2 Daisy wheel printer, drum plotter and laser printer etc.

3 The VDU.

4 A printer that forms one character at a time (e.g. daisy wheel).

5 Laser printer, Xerox printer (like a photocopy machine).
6 Pictures and text are both formed from lots of tiny dots.
7 Near letter quality (almost as good as a professional typewriter).
8 The quality is the same as a professional typewriter.
9 Other printers would be much too slow.
10 They are not versatile enough, can't often do colour and the paper size is too small.
11 It takes up less floor space.
12 Computer output on microfilm.
13 It's very small. Therefore much more text and pictures can be stored.
14 Some use dots which do not give the best quality. Others (e.g. the laser) use continuous lines which gives much better quality.
15 (a) Dot matrix.
(b) Plotter.
(c) Daisy wheel or laser.

Chapter 4

1 To store programs and data.
2 To store programs and data not needed quickly.
3 To store programs and data that are needed immediately.
4 It is very slow and unreliable.
5 Sequential access.
6 A disc revolves quickly. Any data takes a fraction of second to find. A tape must read all previous data before the item of interest.
7 A whole batch of data may be read in from tape in the right order.
8 You go straight to a data item without having to read any others.
9 (a) The DVLC centre at Swansea (Driver and Vehicle Licensing Centre).
(b) A file server for a school network of computers.
(c) A backing store for a word processor.
10 Storing permanent data (e.g. a computerized reference library).
11 RAM – random access memory. ROM – read only memory. EPROM – erasable programmable read only memory.
12 Data is lost if the power is switched off (i.e. it's volatile).
13 Word processors, spelling checkers, computer languages etc.
14 RAM would be affected.

Chapter 5

1

2 A program flowchart shows program details; a systems flowchart shows how the system works as a whole.

3

4 Something that can vary (e.g. average mark in an examination).
5 Usually to show that the end of the data has been reached.
6 They show how a problem is split up into subproblems.
7 Each subproblem can be further split up into subproblems until you are left with problems which are easy to solve.

Chapter 6

1 The solution is not usually exactly what was wanted.
2 Hours worked, tax codes, special deductions etc.
3 Data that tests to see if the system is working. That is, you know the results that should be produced when this data is input.
4 No, you can never be 100 per cent sure.
5 A certain unusual combination of data that has not been put in before is encountered.
6 It is a complex and time-consuming task to write your own software.
7 A BASIC debugging package.

Chapter 7

1 Other people (or yourself) may have to modify them later.
2 The GOTO statement.
3 A self-contained part of a program that can be written separately.
4 (a) They are easier to understand.
(b) Different people can write each module.
5 Writing programs in a modular way, making use of structures and using meaningful variable names etc.
6 The instruction books to explain how the computer and programs work.
7 Without good instructions, the system would be difficult to use.
8 User documentation – simple instructions to the user;
program documentation – to enable a specialist to understand how the programs work so that they could modify them.

Chapter 8

1 A language that is easy to understand and English-like.
2 Other languages have been developed for special purposes.
3 It is easy to use.
4 It is usually interpreted; many other languages are compiled.
5 Each line is examined to see if it is correct before being executed.
6 No checking of syntax is necessary as the program is being run.
7 Interpreters are easy for beginners; compilers produce faster results.
8 FORTRAN and COBOL (scientific and business applications);
PASCAL (structured programming teaching); LOGO (teaching young children how to program).
9 LOGO.
10 COBOL. It will need to be edited and recompiled.

Chapter 9

1 (i) Typing errors on entry of data.
(ii) Syntax errors when developing a program.
(iii) Logical errors when developing a program.
(iv) Hardware errors (i.e. a malfunction of the system).
2 Syntax error (e.g. misspelt keyword) and logical error (e.g. making the program go round a loop for ever).
3 A syntax error is an error which means that the computer does not understand what you have typed in.
4 A logical error is an error in the logic of your program. That is, the computer is doing what it has been told to do, but the answers are still wrong.
5 A logical error.
6 By comparing two different people typing in the same data.
7 Verification – checking two sets of data.
Validation – seeing if data is sensible for its purpose.
8 Check that the day is a number between 1 and 31.
Check that the month is a number between 1 and 12.
Check that the year is a number between 1 and 99.
(More complicated checks could be devised.)
9 16/12/51 may be typed in instead of 17/12/51.
10 A verification and validation check.

Chapter 10

1 The processing of data so that useful information can be got from it.
2 No, but it is usually quicker and more efficient.
3 Using a computer system for data processing.

4 Payroll applications, accounting systems, gas and electricity billing, rates demands etc.

5 Filing cabinets, paper, pens, pencils, calculators etc.

6 (i) It is much quicker.

(ii) It takes less people to operate the system.

(iii) The computer can perform many operations on the data that would have taken too long by hand.

(iv) Offices may be linked together and share the data processing power of a single computer system.

7 Searching, classifying, doing arithmetic, printing reports etc.

8 (i) How much information needs to be stored.

(ii) How quickly it needs to be accessed.

9 A printout showing some statistics from the system (e.g. the number of validation errors or verification errors etc).

10 The results output from the system could be ridiculous.

Chapter 11

1 A base two number consisting of only 1s and 0s.

2 9.

3 A binary digit.

4 A group of eight bits. It is a standard size for much computer hardware.

5 One method is to use the ASCII code.

6 American Standard Code for Information Interchange.

7 66 decimal.

8 An even or odd number of 1s transmitted with each BYTE.

9 Even parity.

10 It is the 'Y'. The code 0 1 0 1 1 0 0 1 should have been sent.

Chapter 12

1 A collection of records with something in common.

2 A file may be organized as shown in the following diagram.

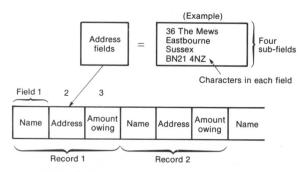

3 The key field is most important because it usually identifies the record.
4 A master file contains the most up-to-date information. A transaction file contains information which can be used to update the master file.

5

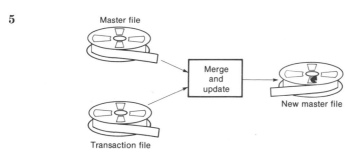

Master file

Merge
and
update

New master file

Transaction file

6 File maintenance means keeping files up to date. It is important if the system is to be useful and efficient.
7 If the files to be merged are in the same order, it makes the merging process more efficient.
8 Making one bigger file from two smaller ones.
9 Serial access means that you have to look at all the data before the item of interest. With random access you do not. Therefore random access is quicker.
10 When jobs are processed in a batch, it can be thought of as a sort of queue. Serial access is ideal for processing things one after the other as in a queue.
11 Random access.
12 Make sure that the write protect mechanism is on.
13 Get the old master file together with the latest transaction file to produce a new master file (grandfather, father and son files).
14 Passwords.

Chapter 13

1 It is easier to use.
2 Binary code consisting of 0s and 1s.
3 It is too tedious and one can easily make lots of errors.
4 An aid to the memory.
5 It consists of lots of mnemonics instead of machine code. Also, the computer can help to find errors in your program etc.
6 A register where data can be temporarily stored inside the CPU.
7 To help all the circuits work together in synchronization.
8 Changing a high level language into a low level language.
9 A low level language designed to help people program the computer.

10 It changes the mnemonics into the machine code that will run on a particular computer.

Chapter 14

1 To make computers easier to use.
2 An operating system that allows jobs to be run one after the other.
3 When a few seconds delay could be fatal (e.g. controlling a missile).
4 Programs to help you do some basic operations such as formatting discs etc.
5 Disc editor, memory checker, printer driver, disc to tape routines.
6 On-line.
7 People don't want to write their own software.
8 Payroll system, graph package, stock control, circuit designer, word processor for micro.
9 (a) Multi-access.
(b) Batch.
(c) Real time.

Chapter 15

1 It is quicker, could take up less space, you can get more information from the system very easily.
2 TV-based information system; weather, news etc.
3 It has two-way communication facilities.
4 Information providers. They put information on to Prestel and other screens.
5 Subscriptions, telephone and some IP charges.
6 Shopping by using the Prestel terminal, for example.
7 It is only a one-way communication process.
8 To transmit computer data over the telephone line.
9 Acoustic coupler – can be used from anywhere with a standard telephone handset.
Modem – not affected when being used in a noisy room.
10 Giving the customer on-screen information such as statements, current balance and the ability to transfer money from one place to another.

Chapter 16

1 Designing a new system for computerization if necessary.
The person (people) in charge of the systems analysis task.
2 Defining the problem, feasibility study, gathering information, analysis, detailed design, implementation. This must also include

writing documentation and training.

3   The problem must be very well defined.

4   A detailed study to see if using computers is a good idea. Otherwise a lot of money may be spent on an unnecessary system.

5   They get information from the people who will use the system and also the people who are trying to work the existing system.

6   After the feasibility study when the go-ahead has been given.

7   The systems flowcharts.

8   Getting the system installed and working.

9   Gathering data to be input to the system.

10   Training is necessary so that people can easily use the system. The systems analysts usually train the managers.

11   To enable people to understand the system, and others to modify the system later.

User and technical documentation are both necessary.

12   Seeing if the system is running OK after a few months.

To see if any bugs have cropped up which need ironing out.

Chapter 17

1   Verifier. Checks to see if data entry staff have entered data correctly. Key to disc operator. Types in data at keyboard so that it is put onto a disc by a special machine.

2   Checks all the paper is in the right place at the right time.

3   A person who writes applications programs such as stock control.

4   Low level language.

5   The systems analysts.

6   The programs are usually very long and complicated. It is too much work for one person.

7   The programmer.

The systems analysts.

8   See page 100.

9   Computers often work 24 hours a day.

Put the paper in printer, keep a log of what the computer is doing, start up the computer in the morning if necessary.

10   (See Chapter 16.)

11   The commissioning engineer.

12   The maintenance engineer.

13   The research engineers and scientists.

14   The systems programmers.

15   Data control clerk, data entry staff.

Chapter 18

1 (a) and (c).
2 (a) Yes to give many different cooking functions.
(b) Yes to display often-used pages of your choice.
(c) Yes to go through a set task.
3 (a) Process control.
(b) They don't get bored, are able to work 24 hours a day, more efficient, more accurate etc.
4 The robots are not versatile enough yet. Also, computers are not powerful enough.
5 (a) Heat/colour sensor and control to switch oven on and off.
(b) Temperature sensor to control a bleeper or light on the dash board of the car.

Chapter 19

1 Bar code reader, laser scanner, POS terminal.
2 Faster, more efficient, other statistics are available. Fewer people are needed, so there may be unemployment; resistance to new technology; a lot of retraining is necesssary.
3 (Project.)
4 See page 112.
5 (Project.)
6 Time sheets (manual entry) and clock cards (automatic entry).
7 Make sure that no one works more than a certain number of hours in a day etc.
8 It's very much quicker.
9 It makes many people redundant.
10 Mars bars and Lego sets!
11 Some items may have been stolen.

Chapter 20

1 CAD, working out weather forecasts and controlling a power station.
2 A system where the computer can give expert answers. See page 118.
3 They can monitor many patients 24 hours a day without getting bored.
4 Building a mathematical model of the bridge union CAD. PERT would also be useful during the construction of the bridge.
5 Project Evaluation Review Techniques. It helps manage very large projects. See page 120.
6 Collecting readings automatically by computer (e.g. weather information).

Collecting all information about the day-to-day running of a nuclear power station.

7 Computer-aided design and computer-aided manufacture.

8 Designing cars and aircraft.

9 Computer-controlled machine tools in a factory.

10 (Project.)

11 (Project.)

12 (Project.)

Chapter 21

1 Computer-aided learning.

2 They help make the students more interested in what is going on. They never get tired like a teacher does etc.

3 (a) Sending out standard letters to parents.

(b) Producing lists.

(c) A computerized notice board.

(d) Automatic examination marking.

4 Reports and exam grades – tutors, housemasters, headmaster etc. Teams and forms – sports teachers finding out what lessons may be missed by a team.

Clubs and societies names and addresses – teachers in charge of activities who may be arranging a school trip.

5 Authors – word processing.

Accountants – spreadsheets.

Clubs – databases of members.

Children – games.

Artists – computer graphics.

6 Lots of extra software and equipment such as printers etc. may be needed.

Artists – extra software to help draw pictures, extra hardware such as digitizer, mouse or light pen etc.

Editor of magazine – word processor and picture drawing facilities, laser printer for camera ready copy etc.

7 Speed of operation, larger memories, better coloured graphics and sound.

Chapter 22

1 Managers not knowing where the cars were in the country.

2 They looked at the problem to see if it could be solved by computers.

3 Modems.

4 Disc. The information may be needed quickly to deal with a customer enquiry.

5 Type of car and registration number – each car must be identified.
Mileage – to know when car is due for a service.
Dates of hire – to know if cars are booked on certain days.
Number in stock at branch – to know where a car may be obtained if needed quickly.

6 A computer terminal and printer plus a modem.

7 Data is checked as it is being entered to see if it is sensible.

8 Date and registration number.

9 A good dot matrix printer with NLQ (near letter quality) mode. It is quick and of good enough quality for customer receipts.

10 Identification of car.

11 No.

12 09/08/90 – when 3 years old.

13 To identify that particular Scorpion.

14 Is the car being used? Is the car in for a service? Who has hired the car?

15 Car type, data needed, date to return, area needed, name of customer.

16 Customer name. This would be used for most enquiries that needed to be dealt with quickly.

17 Perhaps, but certainly no longer. It would take up too much disc space. To estimate size of disc you need to know how many characters are needed for each car, then times by the number of cars that you have. Also use similar method for booking information. Don't forget much software will also have to be stored on disc.

18 Working out wages, word processing and electronic mail.

19 (a) Which cars are used most.

(b) What areas are used most.

(c) How many customers don't get the car they asked for.

(d) How many cars are lying idle etc.

20 On-line. Batch would be too slow.

Chapter 23

1 They are cheaper and more effective.

2 Welding car bodies, typesetting in the newspaper industry, operating petrol pumps and monitoring power stations.

3 At present computers are only powerful enough to cope with specialist tasks.

4 They give people more time; hence they affect their leisure.
Information about people can be obtained from computers.

5 Hospitals, schools, police, councils, banks.

6 Information may be used for the wrong purpose.

7 Information can be got quickly in an emergency.
Government can get statistics easily.
Police could track down criminals more easily.

8 To help them cope with running their business efficiently.
9 They can check to see if information stored about them on computer is correct.
10 Good reasons: Computers won't get bored.
Pupils may learn at any time of day or night.
Bad reasons: No personal contact with people.
Computer can't tell if pupil is working properly!
11 Good reasons: No more counting up items on shelves.
Much less paperwork.
Bad reasons: Not so many people needed.
Computer can monitor how hard people are working!

Chapter 24

1 Computers understanding speech, laser discs storing computer data and very realistic computer graphics.
2 These machines will be able to solve problems without the solution being worked out by a human in the way that is necessary now.
3 (Project.)
4 Computer-aided learning had finally made teachers unnecessary.
Good reasons: Pupils can learn at their own speed.
Computer will spend much time with each pupil without getting fed up.
Bad reasons: They will have no personal relationships.
Pupils will sit in front of screen all day.

Having followed a planned revision programme, you should be well prepared for the examinations and confident of your chances of success. The following advice may help you achieve your best on the day:

1 Get a good night's sleep before the examination. Do not sit up late doing last-minute revision – you will become over-tired.
2 Do not rush around on the morning of an important examination looking for pens and pencils – prepare the night before. Make sure that you have pens, pencils, rulers, perhaps a flowchart template, spare ink, pencil sharpeners etc. Most examination centres require that you take your materials in in a see-through bag.
3 Arrive in good time for the examination.
4 Make sure you know how many questions you must attempt.
5 The number of marks for each question is usually indicated. This will give you some idea of what is required by the examiner. There is no point in spending ages on a question worth only a few marks.
6 Read the questions carefully and make use of all the information that is given you.
7 Do not waste time trying to answer questions you cannot do. Leave them till last but make sure you come back to them.
8 Write clearly using good English.
9 If you finish the examination early, read through what you have written and check your answers.

accumulator   77
acoustic coupler   90
airline bookings   112
American Standard Code for
    Information Interchange   67
analogue information   103
analogue to digital converter   104
applications programmers   100
applications programs   84
arithmetic unit   16
ASCII   67
assemblers   80
assembly languages   79
automatic weather station   121

backing store   15, 32
backup files   74
bar code(s)   21, 111
bar code readers   21
base two   66
BASIC   52
batch operating systems   73
batch processing   33, 73, 83
binary   12, 66
binary digit   67
binary pulse trains   68
bit   67
byte   67

CAD/CAM   122
CAL   125
case studies   130
cassette tape   32
CEEFAX   87
central processing unit   15
character(s)   70
character printers   26
civil engineering
    applications   120
classifying   64
COBOL   52
code   67
COM   30
commissioning engineers   101
compilation   54
compilers   54
computer-aided design   122
computer-aided learning   125

computer games   128
computer music   128
computer operators   100
computer output on
    microfilm   30
computers and society   135
constants   50
control systems   104
control unit   15, 77
CPU   15, 77

Daisy wheel printer   27
data   11
database   86
data capture   19, 94, 113
data controllers   99
data control staff   99
data entry department   22
data entry systems   17
data logging   121
data preparation manager   99
data preparation staff   99
data processing   60
data processing (application)   61
data processing manager   100
debugging packages   45
decimal   66
denary   66
development engineers   101
digital information   103
direct access   34
discs   33
documentation   50, 96
document readers   19
domestic robots   108
dot matrix printer   26
DP department   99
drum plotter   29
dummy data   44

E13B characters   19
EDP   61
educational administration
    applications   125
electronic clock   77
electronic data processing   61
electronic mail   89, 116
electronic office   115

employment (effects of
  computers)   136
encoding   11
EPROM   36
Erasable Programmable Read
  Only Memory   36
errors   56
even parity   68
execute   32
expert systems   118

father file   74
feasibility study   93
feedback   108
fetch   32
fetch – decode – execute cycle   78
file(s)   70
file maintenance   72
file processing   72
file security   74
flatbed plotter   29
floppy discs   34
flowcharts   37
FORTRAN   53
future of computers   139

GEM   82
general purpose language   52
generations of files   74
GOSUBS   48
grandfather file   74
graphical output   29
graphics   27
graphics digitizer   23
graphics environment
  manager   82

hard copy   26
hard disc pack   34
hardware   14
high level languages   52
home computers   127
human error   56
human readable form   17, 19

icon   18
IF THEN statements   48
immediate access store   16, 32

industrial robots   107
information   11
information providers   88
information retrieval
  systems   86
input   11, 15, 17
installation engineers   101
intensive care units   119
interactive   126
interpreters   54
interviews   93
IP   88

keyboard   12, 18
key field   71
key to disc systems   22
key to store systems   22
key to tape systems   22

laser printers   28
laser scanners   21
leisure (effects of
  computers)   136
light pen   23
line printers   26, 28
logging on   88
logical errors   56
LOGO   53
low level languages   76

machine code   78
machine readable form   17, 19, 20
magnetic ink character
  recognition   19
magnetic tape   32
mailbox   89
mainframe computers   14
main store   15, 32, 36
maintenance engineers   101
manual data processing   60
mark sense readers   19
master files   74
medical applications   118
memory   14, 35
memory location   79
merging   72
MICR   19
MICR reader   19

microcomputer(s)   12
microfiche   30
microfiche reader   30
microprocessor   12, 106
MIDI   128
minicomputer   12
mnemonics   79
modem   90
modules   47
mouse   17
multi-user operating system   82
musical instrument digital
    interface   128

near letter quality   27
network operating systems   83
NLQ   27

OCR   20
odd parity   69
off-line   83
on-line operating system   83
operating systems   81
operations manager   100
operations staff   100
optical character recognition   20
optical discs   35
Oracle   87
output   11
output of data   25

packages   45
page printers   26, 28
parity   68
parity check   68
Pascal   53
passwords   75
payroll systems   113
PERT   120
plotter   29
point of sale (POS)
    terminals   111
Prestel   88
privacy (effects of
    computers)   137
printed lists   64
problems (defining)   92
procedures   48

process control   104
processing   15
processing of information   11, 15
program(s)   14
program flowcharts   39
programmer   99
programming   46
programming errors   56
programming staff   99
Project Evaluation Review
    Techniques   120

quinkey   19

RAM   36
random access   32
random access (files)   73
random access memory   36
read only disc   36
read only memory   36
real time systems   84
records   70
repeat until loops   49
reports   64
research engineers and
    scientists   101
robotics   106
rogue values   39
ROM   36

searching   64
searching (files)   73
security   74
sequential access   32
sequential access (files)   73
serial access   73
serial printers   26
shift leader   100
simulations   124
social effects of computers   138
soft copy   25
software   14
software development
    engineers   101
software houses   84
solving problems   42
son file   74
sorting   72

sorting (files)   73
speech   24
speech output   30
speech recognition   141
spelling checkers   115
stock control   111
storing   64
structure(s)   48
structure diagrams   40
syntax errors   54, 56
systems analysis   92, 100
systems analyst   93
systems flowcharts   40
systems programmers   100

technical and research staff   101
technical documentation   50, 96
teleshopping   89
Teletext   87
testing solutions to problems   44
thinking computers   141
toolkits   45
touch screen   24
transaction files   74
turnaround documents   20

updating   72
user documentation   50, 96
user friendly   82
utilities   84

validation   58
variables   39, 50
VDU   30
verification   58
visual display unit   30

while do structure   50
Winchester disc   34
word processing   115